Roger,

You're a winner!

Art Garner

WHY
WINNERS
W#1N

WHY WINNERS WIN

#1

ART GARNER

PELICAN PUBLISHING COMPANY
Gretna 1998

First edition, April 1981
Second printing, November 1982
Third printing, September 1985
Second edition, September 1995
Fifth printing, April 1998

The word "Pelican" and the depiction of a pelican
are trademarks of Pelican Publishing Company, Inc.,
and are registered in the U.S. Patent and Trademark Office.

Library of Congress Cataloging-in-Publication Data

Garner, Art.
    Why winners win / Art Garner. — 2nd ed.
      p. cm.
    ISBN 1-56554-148-0
    1. Success—Psychological aspects.   I. Title.
BF637.S8G356 1995
158'.1—dc20   95-2872
                                  CIP

Manufactured in the United States of America

Published by Pelican Publishing Company, Inc.
P.O. Box 3110, Gretna, Louisiana 70054-3110

This book is affectionately dedicated to:

My wife, Ann, who has been my constant supporter and source of encouragement when I needed it the most. Her assistance with researching, editing, and typing this book has been invaluable. As a real winner, she always demonstrates a high level of motivation to achieve the goals we have set together.

My son, Alan, who has brought me so many years of enjoyment and happiness in watching him grow up to be a positive and contributing young professional. His level of maturity far exceeds his years. His gentle spirit and kind demeanor are traits that complement his personality.

My daughter, Kim, who has provided me with so many smiles and joys as I watched her develop from a little girl in "pigtails" into a mature and loving young woman. Her keen insights and warm personality brought laughter into our home.

My daughter-in-law, Alice Cartwright Garner, who has demonstrated her love and her desire to make this world better by helping others.

My grandson, Alexander Cartwright Garner, for bringing so much love, enjoyment, and excitement into my life. I'm confident that he is the world's best grandson! I'm amazed at his beauty, his level of intelligence, and the awareness with which he views this complex world.

Contents

Acknowledgments

It is very difficult, if not virtually impossible, for a writer to identify all the people who have influenced his or her personal and professional life.

Teachers, coaches, supervisors, administrators, colleagues, ministers, friends, relatives, and my family have taught me so many valuable lessons. Their patience and humanistic concern stimulated me to continue my efforts toward a self-actualizing life. They saw and encouraged the development of things in me that I was unable to perceive. My life has been richer and more exciting because of their faith in my potential.

The author wishes to express his gratitude to Barbara Fitzpatrick for her assistance in typing and editing this book, and to my favorite college student, Dr. Estelle Helm, who has carefully edited the final copy of this book and provided me with many hours of inspiration and assistance. Dr. Helm taught me more as a student in my classes than I taught her.

Special thanks goes to my wife, Ann, for the years of encouragement and devotion she has given me. Her words of praise were available and given when I needed them the most. I am also indebted to our children, Alan and Kim, for the years of enjoyment and love they have provided. Their interest in "Dad's work" always filled me with pride.

Above all, I am grateful to the Lord for the strength to begin and complete this task. His grace and strength have given me the mental, physical, and spiritual energy necessary for this challenge.

I hope you will enjoy reading this book as much as I have enjoyed writing it. I trust that it will stimulate you to make any appropriate and necessary changes to enrich your life. Your success depends on what *you* can get out of *you!* The time you spend reading this book will have been well invested if an illustration, quotation, principle, concept, or anecdote helps you actualize more of the potential God has given you.

May your path be filled with many opportunities to help others!

WHY
WINNERS
W🏆N

CHAPTER 1

Your Most Important Quality

"Every adversity carries with it the seed of an equivalent or greater benefit."

NAPOLEON HILL

Several years ago a young boy saw a "Help Wanted" sign in the window of the drugstore in his home town. He went in and asked to see the owner. "I'd like to check on the job you have advertised in the window," he said.

"Fine," said the druggist. "We need someone to help us in our business." He told the boy they needed someone to make deliveries to customers who telephoned their orders to the drugstore.

The young boy said, "I have six questions I want to ask you."

The druggist replied, "Very well; ask them."

"First," the boy said, "I want to know how much you pay. Then I want to know what kind of health insurance program you provide. I want to find out how many days of vacation time I'll get each year. Then tell me how many holidays and sick days you provide annually. And how much

13

time do I get off for lunch every day? And I have one more question."

"Fine," the druggist said. "I'm glad to answer all your questions."

"Well," the boy remarked, "I want to know if you have a bicycle I can ride to deliver the orders."

The druggist responded, "No, I'm sorry. We don't have a bicycle."

The boy quickly countered, "Well, you can forget it. I wouldn't have this job." And he walked out in a huff.

About two hours later another young boy walked by and saw the "Help Wanted" sign. He walked in with a big smile and asked to see the boss. A clerk pointed toward the druggist, and the boy went to the back of the store and waited patiently while the druggist filled a prescription for a customer. He then introduced himself and said he wanted the job. The druggist said, "Well, don't you want to know how much we pay?"

"No sir," the boy replied, "because you look like an honest man who will treat me fairly." The boy continued, "You see, sir, my mother is out of work, and we need the money, so I'm ready to start working right now."

The druggist said to the young boy, "I've just got to tell you about a boy who came in about two hours ago who also wanted this job. He had six questions which he asked me, and I answered each of them quite honestly for him. His last question was, 'Do you have a bicycle I can ride to deliver the orders?' I told him we didn't have one, and he walked out of the store after telling me he wouldn't have this job. I was very truthful with him. You see, we don't have a bicycle, but we do have a new station wagon you can use to make the deliveries."

What was the difference in the two boys? When we discover *that* difference, we have identified what it takes to be a WINNER. We have discovered the most important thing about every human being. It easily separates the WINNERS from those who wish they were.

One of my favorite stories is the one about the fellow who wanted to learn how to jump from an airplane and parachute safely to earth. During the instruction period the jumpmaster showed him how to strap the parachute on his back and how to make it open properly. The instructor told him, "When you hear the signal to jump, jump away from the plane and count to ten before you pull the rip cord. And if the chute doesn't open, pull the ring on the emergency cord. The parachute will open, and you'll float safely to earth, where a jeep will be waiting to take you back to the airport."

At eight o'clock the next morning the fellow was at the airport—ready for his first jump. He strapped the parachute on and climbed into the airplane. He stood in the door of the plane as the pilot flew over the jump site. The jumpmaster signaled for him to jump. The fellow took a deep breath and hit the air. He quickly counted: one

one-thousand, two one-thousand, three one-thousand, and up to ten one-thousand. Then he pulled the rip cord. Nothing happened. So he pulled the emergency cord—quickly. And nothing happened. He said, "Yeah, and I bet the jeep's not down there either."

This little story is meaningful because it places a unique emphasis on the importance of the winning concept in the story about the boy looking for a job at the drugstore. What do you think this important characteristic is? It's so important that I can hardly wait to share it with you. I've seen it enrich the lives of thousands of people. I have watched it transform the lives of those who have enrolled in classes I teach on motivation and personal achievement. This powerful attribute can turn your life around also. It happens every day in America. It can transform you into the kind of person you have always wanted to become. It really is the most important thing about you.

It thrills me that you are reading this book. It tells me that you want to enrich your personal and professional life. I love to see people change their lives and become more productive, because I know they will be much happier and will enjoy fulfilling lives.

A school administrator told me how a little first-grade boy fell down the steps of a school bus one morning and skinned his legs. During the morning recess the little fellow ran into another boy on the playground and knocked two teeth out. After lunch the little fellow was running outside on the pavement and fell and broke his arm. After the principal had taken him to the hospital where the boy's arm was placed in a cast, he decided to take the boy home before he was injured again. While driving him home, the principal noticed that the boy was holding something in his hand. He asked him what it was. The boy smiled and showed him a quarter he had in his tight little fist and said, "You know, Dr. Perritt, I've never found a quarter before. This is the luckiest day of my life!"

I'd say this little fellow is going to continue to be a WINNER in life because he is demonstrating that rare quality which is so necessary to be a WINNER. And *you* have this important quality also—at least to some degree. This book will help you develop this characteristic to a much greater extent. It will cause others to be drawn magnetically to you. I know you're on the right road. You're reading this book. The only people who read books like this one are those who want to "grow and glow." As a friend of mine says, "When you're green you grow, and when you're ripe you rot."

There's a beautiful story about a farmer who had lived on an old, broken-down farm all his life. The rain had washed gullies all through it, the trees were of little value for pulpwood, the farmhouse and barn looked like shacks, and the whole mess was located several miles from the main highway. So he decided to sell it all. He got in his old pick-up truck and drove to the newspaper office. He went in and told the secretary he wanted to run an ad in the paper to sell his place. She sent the farmer back to talk to the copywriter, who listened to him very carefully and then wrote the ad. It emphasized the beautiful rolling hills and the babbling brooks—not the gullies. It spoke of the variety of trees that enhanced the landscape and the possibilities of restoring the home according to one's own personal taste. And it talked about the secluded location where one could enjoy hearing the birds and smelling the lovely honey-suckles. The ad didn't mention the desolate location.

The copywriter read the ad to the farmer. He said, "Would you please read it to me again?" And he asked for still another reading. After hearing it a third time, the farmer walked over, picked up the piece of paper and said, "Now you look here, fellow, this farm ain't for sale. That's exactly the kind of place I've been wanting all my life!"

The farmer had lived for sixty years on that land. What caused him to have a different picture of the situation? It's all a matter of *attitude,* isn't it? And that's what this chapter is about. I fully agree with the adage, "Our attitude determines our altitude." Nothing is more important than our attitude. It separates the WINNERS from the losers.

The Stanford Research Institute conducted a study which concluded that twelve percent of our success depends on our knowledge and technical skills and eighty-eight percent on our ability to manage interpersonal relationships successfully. This implies a positive attitude, cooperation, enthusiasm, and commitment.

Talent is relatively inexpensive. You can buy it almost anywhere. Just think of the number of talented college football players who are never invited to try out for a professional team. Think, too, of the outstanding collegiate basketball players, baseball players, golfers, tennis players, and talented individuals in other sports who never make it to the "big leagues."

Look at the number of talented actresses, accountants, students who would like to enter medical school, teachers who want to teach, and a host of others who are refused admittance into their preferred fields. You see, talent is inexpensive.

Education is also relatively inexpensive. It is easier to become educated in America today than ever before. Any student who really wants to can get an education. Scholarships, loans, part-time jobs, and grants are available to needy and worthy students.

There's one thing, however, that you can't buy, even for a million dollars. And that is a positive attitude. It just isn't for sale. It comes from within.

Our society has witnessed tremendous and sometimes almost unbelievable scientific accomplishments. Space explorations continue to escalate. Medical researchers are probing into areas which they believe will provide answers to important health questions. Their answers will result in more comfortable living and longer lives.

Knowledge doubled for the first time in 1750, the second time in 1900, the third time in 1950, and the fourth time in 1960, and it presently doubles every five years. Research continues to probe deeper into areas little known to us only a few years ago. There have been more books published in the past twenty-five years than in the previous five hundred.

More than half of the jobs available to a young man today were not even in existence when his father was a boy. In fact, ninety percent of all scientists and technologists who have ever lived are alive now.

Monumental achievements have amazed us. But the greatest discovery of all concerns man himself. One of my favorite quotations is from the psychologist William James: "The greatest discovery of my generation is that human beings can alter their lives by altering their attitudes of mind."

WINNERS believe that something good can emerge from every situation, even though they cannot see it at the moment. That's where faith starts to work. I like the story of the rich father who wanted to ascertain the attitudes of his twin boys. He gave one of them a large pile of presents. The boy began complaining about the colors, the sizes, the shapes. To the other son the father gave a large pile of manure. This boy began singing, whistling, and shoveling the manure.

He looked up and said, "With a pile of manure this high, there's got to be a pony in here somewhere!"

This fellow is a WINNER. He'll make it in life. He has captured the spirit which Napoleon Hill suggested in the inspiring statement that "every adversity contains the seed of an equivalent or greater benefit." This success principle conveys the message that every cloud has a silver lining. We may not be able to see it, but it's there.

One evening on the way home from his office, Matthew Henry was robbed. Before going to bed, he wrote in his diary, "Let me be thankful, first, because I was never robbed before; second, because although they took my purse, they did not take my life; third, because although they took my all, it was not much; and fourth, because it was I who was robbed, not I who robbed."

A friend was telling me about an incident in the airport in Dallas. He saw this young boy in a wheelchair, smiling from ear to ear. He decided to visit with the boy, who was apparently waiting for his mother to return with some food. He asked the boy if he had been in a wheelchair all his life. The young fellow looked up at him with a refreshing warmth and said, "Not yet I ain't, Mister!" I don't know how long he had been crippled, but I do know he had a positive belief that some day he would be better. Don't you imagine that this attitude helped him smile a great deal each day?

One of the most rewarding experiences of my

life happened the day I met Ed Dohrman in Atlantic City. I was there to conduct a workshop for the annual meeting of the New Jersey Society of Radiologic Technologists. While I was checking into the hotel, Mary Vahey, the conference chairperson, walked over and invited me to have dinner with her and four others. After taking my luggage to the room, I met them in the lobby. Mary introduced me to Ed Dohrman and his seeing-eye dog, Yetta. I'll never forget that meeting and the next two days I spent with Ed.

There are many beautiful people in this world, and my traveling allows me to meet quite a few of them. While we were eating at Zaberer's Restaurant that night, I met another beautiful person—Janet, the efficient waitress who served our table. Noticing that Ed was blind, when she served his dinner, she whispered softly to him, "Your steak is at four o'clock, your peas at seven o'clock, and your potato at eleven o'clock." Her sensitivity to him prompted me to write a letter of appreciation to the manager of the restaurant complimenting her caring attitude.

The next morning I was waiting for the elevator on the fifth floor. When it stopped and the doors opened, I said, "Hello, Yetta."

Ed responded, "Good morning, Art. How are you? Isn't it a beautiful day?"

I replied, "Yes, Ed, it surely is. May I buy your breakfast?"

He replied, "I'd like that. But first I must meet

Yetta's needs." We walked slowly around the block while Yetta paused periodically.

After we ordered breakfast, I decided it was time to ask Ed how he was able to maintain such a beautiful attitude toward life. He told me his story. It moved me. Ed had been a radiologic technologist working in a large hospital. He had been in good health, enjoying his work. Diabetes caused him to lose his eyesight at the age of thirty-seven. Shortly after that his kidneys failed. Ed never gave up. He believed tomorrow would be better. His failing health necessitated a kidney transplant. Although the new kidney failed a few times, it did eventually function.

Ed was unable to learn to read braille because the diabetes had impaired his fingertip sensitivity. This stimulated him to spend his spare time listening to tapes. Ed had learned that "every adversity contains the seed of an equivalent or greater benefit."

While we were eating breakfast, Ed related the philosophy which helped him maintain a refreshing attitude toward life in the midst of difficult circumstances. He said, "Art, I decided when I lost my eyesight that I could be bitter, and no one would enjoy being around me. Or, I could be positive and try to encourage others. I'm glad I chose to be positive." I noticed during the convention that people were always standing around him. His smile warmed many hearts.

Three months later the phone rang one night

about ten o'clock at our home. When I answered it, it was Ed. "Hello, Art," he greeted me. "What's happening in your life these days that is exciting?" After we had chatted for a few minutes, I asked him what he had been doing lately. He replied, "Well, today I mowed the lawn."

I said, "Ed, you're blind. How in the world did you mow the lawn?"

He said, "I put a milk can at one end of the yard and another one at the other end. Then I tied a rope between them to give me some direction while I mowed."

I asked him what else he had been doing. He replied, "Well, last week I painted one side of the house in which we're now living.

I replied, "Ed, how many times does someone have to tell you that you're blind?"

He laughed and said, "If you keep painting over the same general section, you're bound to cover it all. When my wife, Barbara, came home she said I had more paint on me than I had on the house."

He then told me he had just completed building some shelves. He was a little disappointed that the shelves were one-eighth of an inch lower on one end. He had also been chopping wood for the fireplace.

A couple of months later, I telephoned Ed. I asked him what he was doing to enjoy life. He told me he had been riding his bicycle. I said, "Ed, what if you run off into a ditch?"

He replied, "Well, then I'll know I've gone too

far to the right." Oh, what a beautiful attitude, I thought.

Ed and I often corresponded over the following months. Barbara said he loved to walk to the mailbox and feel several letters in there. Every time I've used Ed's life as an illustration in one of my speeches, I've asked twenty-five listeners to write him notes of encouragement. One time Barbara told me that these letters helped keep him going. He couldn't wait for her to get home from work to read them to him.

One Sunday night I kept telephoning their home, but no one answered. Finally, about midnight, Barbara answered the phone. She told me that Ed had been taken in serious condition to the hospital in Albany, New York. Monday evening I called the hospital and talked to Ed. He said, "Art, it will be a while before I write you. This morning the surgeons had to amputate my right arm. But I'm going to learn to write with my left hand now." Tears filled my eyes as I thought of my lovely friend who was suffering greatly but still maintaining a refreshing attitude toward life.

Ed died the next morning. Along with a lot of other people, I'm a different and better person because of Ed Dohrman. He was a real WINNER.

Obstacles can be a WINNER'S steppingstones to greatness. For example, Demosthenes, the great orator, had a speech impediment which he conquered by placing pebbles in his mouth and shouting. Beethoven, one of the world's greatest composers, was deaf. Milton, the great poet, was blind. Abraham Lincoln was almost completely self-educated. The Wright brothers were bicycle mechanics by trade, not scientists. Winston Churchill overcame a speech impediment to become one of this century's greatest orators. Helen Keller, blind and deaf, became one of the great women of our nation and was admired throughout the world.

When I was in San Francisco recently, I boarded an elevator operated by Walter Henley, who was singing and whistling. A lady asked him why he was so happy. He smiled and said, "Because I have never lived this day before."

A negative thinker has the attitude of the old farmer who walked with his wife down to the train station to see their first train. When the farmer saw how large and heavy the engine was, he said, "They'll never get that thing to move." In a few minutes the engineer boarded, and the train started moving down the track. The old farmer looked at his wife and said, "Well, I'll tell you one thing. They'll never get it stopped." This old fellow had made up his mind to be negative—regardless.

Sometimes we may feel like my good friend, David Stone, who lives in Palm Springs, California. At the conclusion of a workshop I was conducting for the Loma Linda University Medical Center, David stopped by a clock shop to buy his wife, Nellie, a grandfather clock for her birthday. After paying for the large clock, he asked that it be delivered to his home that afternoon. The owner said it would be impossible because the shop was behind with its deliveries.

David said, "O.K., strap it on my back!"

The owner replied, "What? You're out of your mind! The clock is too heavy."

David said, "I paid for the clock. It's mine. Tie it on my back."

Reluctantly the shopkeeper strapped it on his back, and David started walking home. About three blocks down the street a drunk came out of a bar, ran into David, and knocked him down to the sidewalk. The clock lay broken in a hundred pieces all over the pavement. David stood up and said to the drunk, "Why don't you look where you are going?"

The drunk looked up at him and said, "Why don't you wear a wrist watch like normal people do?"

Someone said that all men are created equal, but it's what they do afterward that makes the difference. An individual's attitude determines to what extent he will develop his talents and in which direction he points his life. I've always been impressed by the philosophy of Oliver Wendell Holmes, who said, "The most important thing about a person is not where he stands, but in which direction he is moving."

Dad and Mother believed they could help make America a strong nation by rearing their children, attending church, supporting their city, and working hard at their jobs. During World War II both of them worked twelve hours a night, seven nights a week to provide for our family. After working all night on Friday, Mother would prepare breakfast, and Dad would take my brother and me fishing on Saturday mornings.

Mother always had a great deal of faith—in God, us, people, jobs, school, and the future. She truly believed that each of us could take the talents God had given us and become the kind of person each wanted to become. She believed that success depended on a positive and persistent attitude.

A WINNER closes the doors on past failures. By viewing our temporary setbacks as stepping-stones rather than stumbling blocks, we can build the kind of personal future that will be satisfying and rewarding. It's what we bring to life, not what life brings to us that counts.

Each morning brings us a fresh, new day. We can make of it what we will. The WINNER gets up each morning on the right side of the mind. He knows that the attitude he adopts early each morning determines the kind of day he will have. During the day he notices that attitude begets atmosphere.

Recently I was enjoying a cup of hot tea while reading the newspaper early one morning. Our daughter, Kim, came through the room, looked at me, and asked, "How do you feel this morning, Dad?"

"Wonderful, Kim," I said.

She responded, "Well, why don't you notify your face?"

Wow! Did I get the point! Now when I hear her getting out of bed and walking down the hall, I start smiling.

A WINNER knows that his attitude toward losing determines how long it will be until he wins. David Schwartz relates the story of a WINNER with a positive attitude. Benjamin Fairless, former chief executive of the U.S. Steel Corporation, suggests how we should think when things don't go our way. He said, "It depends on how you look at things. For example, I never had a teacher I hated. Naturally, I was disciplined just like every other pupil, but I always figured it was my own fault that the discipline was necessary. I have also liked every boss I ever had. I always tried to please him and do more than he expected if I possibly could, never less. I have had some disappointments, times when I greatly wanted a promotion and somebody else got it. But I never figured that I was the victim of office politics or bad judgment on the boss's part. Instead of sulking or quitting in a huff, I reasoned things out. Obviously the other fellow deserved the promotion more than I did. What could I do to make myself more deserving of the next opportunity? At the same time I never got angry with myself for losing and never wasted any time berating myself. I was determined to be persistent in the pursuit of my goals."

I'm very much inspired by the story of Steve Walle, a third-grade student at Cold Springs School in Missoula, Montana. The teacher asked

the students to write something about Thanksgiving week for which they were really thankful.
Steve's paper read: "Thanksgiving is special because I get to go to my grandmother's house. She
always has a meal waiting for us. She has some
turkey and some mashed potatoes. My grandfather is nice and so is my grandmother. My
grandfather is a mechanic. He works on tractors
and drives college kids on the bus. They live three
blocks from a candy store. They have a big house.
I am thankful for being alive. I got run over about
three years ago, and lost my sight. And I'm lucky
to be here." His beautiful and heart-warming
story was written in braille.

Millie Nye was in a personal enrichment class I
taught recently. She shared some experiences
which taught each of us a memorable lesson
about thinking and acting positively. One of her
days went something like this: When she got up
one morning, she saw the toilet overflowing.
Later she learned that her daughter had locked
the keys inside the car. That evening she noticed
the roof was leaking. The clothes dryer also broke
that night. And another daughter accidentally
broke a window in the house. All of this in one
day!

Positive-thinking Millie took each of these
thorny problems *one at a time* and did something
constructive about them. At the end of that day
she concluded, "I have no reason not to be
positive."

What a fantastic attitude. She is a WINNER.

Millie had previously faced problems that few people confront in a lifetime. As a child, she lived in a series of foster homes and was eventually placed with Mr. and Mrs. Martin. She had three eye operations, as well as a constant struggle with asthma, but she turned into a smiling little girl because of the tender, loving care of the Martins.

She married a man whom she respected but did not love. That marriage failed after a daughter and son were born. She married a second time for love. Her husband, however, could not handle the responsibilities of marriage and parenthood. Left with three children to rear, she had difficulty with bad health and trouble finding work.

She now has a job she likes and feels that she will someday be an asset to the company. Don't you like her attitude? She wants not just a job, but an opportunity to be useful.

She feels life is too precious to take for granted. She appreciates her life now because of the obstacles she has overcome. She is thankful for her three normal, happy children. She feels a strong will and optimistic attitude will help her through future problems. She has truly made stepping-stones out of obstacles.

Which of the three in the following story would you want to hire to build you a new house? A reporter went out to a place where a construction company was erecting a large new building. She asked the first worker she saw what he was doing. He replied, "Laying brick." She came upon a second worker and asked him what he was doing. He responded, "Earning $7.50 an hour." And when she saw a third construction worker, she asked him the same question. His response was, "I'm building the world's greatest cathedral." I know which of these workers you would want— the same one I would. We'd want the fellow who takes pride in his work. He is the one who enjoys many self-actualizing experiences at work. He probably smiles, whistles, and sings at work, even if he sings to himself. His attitude and quality of work indicate that he is a WINNER.

You probably want to avoid being like the hypochondriac who died in Purdy, Tennessee. He left a note instructing the owner of a monument company to put this epitaph on his gravestone: "I told you people I was sick, and you wouldn't believe me."

WINNERS avoid criticizing, condemning, and complaining. They realize that when you're slinging mud you're losing ground. Losers spend a lot of time cutting others and themselves down. We have often heard that misery loves company. Some people criticize others in their attempt to bring them down to their own level.

There was a beginning teacher in Illinois who fell in love with teaching during her first year in the classroom. Because the school principal had not visited her classroom to evaluate her teaching skills, she assumed that she would not be employed the following year. At the end of the school year she took her materials to the office and prepared to say goodbye. The principal saw her and said, "We have enjoyed having you here this year and look forward to having you teach with us again next year."

She was quite surprised and replied, "Well, I haven't received a contract to teach next year, so I just assumed that you thought I had done a poor job and didn't want me back."

The principal said, "We really want you back. Your students have scored higher on their achievement tests than any of our other students in the last ten years. You've got to come back next year."

The teacher said, "It's easy to teach when you have such a great group of kids as I had. They were sharp, interested, motivated, and all of them had I.Q.'s of 150, 152, 153, and even higher." The principal asked how she knew that the students had such high I.Q. scores. She mentioned the materials he had given her at the beginning of the school year which contained a sheet of paper with the students' names and I.Q. scores on it. He smiled at her and said, "Those were their locker numbers."

Because she thought the students had high I.Q. scores, she had treated them all year as if they did. Her attitude was one of high expectations. She believed in the students. She *knew* they could accomplish the work. Her experience underscores the point that "attitudes are more important than facts."

My friend Helyn Yorke shared a beautiful

story with me. It was a letter written by a fourteen-year-old boy to an administrator at the Massachusetts Institute of Technology. It read:

> M.I.T. is my big aim. Besides receiving A's in algebra, I read everything I can lay my eyes on in all phases of the field of space and science, and go without shoes to save money. I need additional information about tuition, scholarships, and careers in space exploration and rocket engineering.
>
> "I am third in line of a family of five expensive, hungry children; and my father is a lobster fisherman. This adds up to the fact that what becomes of me will depend on me mostly.
>
> "Do you have any advice, so that every minute will count in the next three and a half years? I am coming to M.I.T. somehow, and you will be glad to see me.

I strongly suspect this young lad will continue to be a WINNER the rest of his life. He knows what he wants to do. He knows where he wants to go. He is searching for advice from the right sources to help him achieve his goals. His attitude is refreshing.

We can significantly enhance our relationships with others by imagining that each person we meet is wearing a sign around his or her neck which says, "Please make me feel important." And what does it take to make him feel important? Simply talk in terms of things which interest him, and he'll love being around you. Instead of asking questions which require a yes or no response, use the words *how, who, why, when, what,* and *where* to stimulate responses. For example, instead of asking, "Do you like your work?" ask, "What motivated you to go into this line of work?" In other words, you are talking the other person's language. Everybody loves to talk about himself. Being a good conversationalist makes you a WINNER.

You have noticed that WINNERS are good listeners. In our rapidly moving and highly advanced technological society, it is sometimes difficult to get someone to listen to you. Most people seem to be in a hurry. One can listen with interest by looking directly in the person's eyes while he is speaking or listening, really concentrating on what the person is saying and the meaning it connotes. It is also very helpful to watch the person's nonverbal body language and the messages conveyed.

I've also noticed that WINNERS are frog kissers. That's right—they kiss frogs! (I'll explain this later.) Have you ever felt like a frog? You know, it's when you have the "dropsies," and you wish you had the "upsies." It's when you want to feel energetic, but you feel fatigued; when you are lonesome but wish you had warm companionship; when you are being criticized but wish you were being praised; when you are selfish but wish very much that you were a giver; when you are not sensitive to the needs of others but wish you were a caring and concerned person; when you have procrastinated and are behind in your work but wish you were caught up; and when you are frightened but wish you had a strong faith.

My third-grade teacher, Mrs. Elsie Mae Dorsett, told us one time about a prince who was turned into a frog by a wicked old witch. The only way he could become a prince again was for some beautiful maiden to come by and kiss him. And, by and by, a miracle did happen in his life, just as it can in ours, and a lovely maiden came by and kissed the frog, and he turned back into a handsome prince. Obviously they lived together happily ever after.

Two college girls were at a park when a handsome frog came hopping up to them. He had such a friendly, pleading look that they took him back to the dormitory with them. There they fed and petted him. He responded with such gratitude that one of them leaned over and kissed him. He instantly changed into a handsome young man!

Do you believe that story? The dormitory matron didn't.

Words of praise have changed the lives of many frog-type people. Praise has the power to inspire others to reach just a little higher. You've probably noticed that a word or two of praise can bring joy that lasts for days.

The famous psychologist, William James, wrote, "The deepest principle of human nature is the craving to be appreciated." I suppose each person reading this book remembers a depressing time when he or she did something which he believed deserved recognition or reward, and didn't receive it. This indicates that praise is the greatest payment to receive for a job well done. It usually inspires us to reach a little higher in developing our skills. It also increases our morale, and we're more productive as a result. That's because a little bit of praising always does some spirit-raising.

WINNERS are careful to avoid deflating another person's ego. Lord Chesterfield gave his son some superb advice when his son asked, "How can I make people like me?"

"My son," Chesterfield explained, "make other people like themselves a little better, and I promise you this: they will like you very much."

We may as well admit it: we want people to like us. And the person who says he doesn't care if people like him will be less than truthful about other things also. To be liked is a psychological need each of us has.

We are contributing a great deal to a person's happiness and success when we express genuine appreciation. Such a gesture is particularly rewarding when we compliment an action or specific behavior the person has demonstrated. "Your tie really matches your suit well," or "That lemon icebox pie really satisfied my taste buds" are more meaningful than "You look great," or "That was a great meal."

Participants in the workshops I conduct on human resources development often ask me to suggest some guidelines to help them express appreciation to others. Over the past several years I have offered the following guidelines:

1. Search for things that are close at hand. Quite often we are looking in the distance to see something for which we should express appreciation. This habit causes us to over-look many lovely experiences and opportunities that are close to us.

2. Search for little things to praise. It doesn't have to be an earth-shaking experience or phenomenal discovery or invention to deserve praise. There aren't too many of these happening every day. You may wish to set a goal of finding two or three specific things each day to compliment.

3. Look for the right moment to express your appreciation. Usually the right moment is as soon as possible. The longer we wait to compliment the specific trait or action of the individual, the less powerful it will be. These comments will serve as positive re-inforcement for the individual to replicate his or her performance.

In most cases it is usually quite meaningful to express your appreciation to the individual in front of others. This approach can multiply the effectiveness of your comments. However, in some cases it will be more useful to share your comments privately. For example, if your remarks would cause jealousy or friction, you'd want to approach the person when he or she is alone.

It is very effective to write someone a letter or

note expressing your sincere appreciation. I have found it very useful to keep several blank note cards and envelopes in my attaché cases in my desk at home and at the office, and in my car. Frequently I write notes while I'm at airports, visiting a doctor's office, or even attending faculty meetings. By having stationery with me, I don't have a good excuse for not writing. In fact, one Friday afternoon during a three-hour faculty meeting I wrote thirteen notes of appreciation. It was one of the most productive faculty meetings I ever attended.

Sometimes people we have never met can inspire us immensely. It happened to me one morning when I was in Atlanta to deliver a speech. As I was walking from my hotel room toward the elevator, I followed a well-dressed man down the hall. He stopped by a lady who was pushing a cleaning cart and said, "Good morning. I'm Bob Straw and I just want you to know how much I enjoyed sleeping in that clean room last night. The sheets were clean and I enjoyed the comfortable bed. And it was nice to take a shower in the clean bathroom. I hope you have a nice day."

I have a question for you. Do you think that lady cleaned all those rooms with more enthusiasm that day? Since that morning I have never passed anyone pushing a cleaning cart in a hotel or motel without saying something like that to her. If you have a second hand on your watch, you'll notice it takes only fifteen seconds to repeat what Bob Straw told the lady.

A few years ago someone suggested that "you can tell a great man by the way he treats little people." I've made an effort to observe the leadership styles of individuals at various levels in the management hierarchy. Invariably, those who treat others with respect and dignity motivate their employees to achieve higher goals, perform more efficiently, and have higher morale. Dr. Billy M. Jones, former president of Memphis State University, is an example of a leader who treats others the way he'd want to be treated. Every human being is important to him. He continually expresses appreciation to faculty members, administrators, the staff, and the community for their contributions to the university.

A real WINNER is someone who makes winners out of others. He is like the person described by George Bernard Shaw in *Pygmalion*. Eliza Doolittle says to Colonel Pickering: "You see, really and truly, apart from the things anyone can pick up, such as dressing and speaking, the difference between a lady and a flower girl is not how she behaves, but how she's treated. I shall always be a flower girl to Professor Higgins, because he always treats me as a flower girl and always will; but I know I can be a lady to you, because you always treat me as a lady and always will."

This little rhyme amplifies what Eliza was saying:

> *To sell Don Luther*
> *What Don Luther buys,*

You'd better see Don Luther
Through Don Luther's eyes.

This applies if we are selling cars, houses, insurance, services, ideas, or a marriage proposal. We'll be much more effective when we can see things from the other person's vantage point. Successful sales people know the value of projecting this kind of attitude.

It always excites me to read about people who develop and maintain a positive attitude toward circumstances and people. I love the story which reflects Abraham Lincoln's sensitive heart. It occurred in 1863, when he was busy trying to reunite a divided country. Each day his life was filled with decisions to be made which affected the lives of thousands of people. The easy decisions were made by his staff. He made the tough ones.

A soldier was sentenced to die because he had fallen asleep on guard duty one night. The boy's mother wrote to President Lincoln for help. Lincoln was extremely busy. He could have assigned the task to a subordinate, and no one would have blamed him for doing so. But he investigated the details surrounding the soldier's performance and learned that the boy had been on guard duty for forty-eight hours without any relief. He immediately issued a pardon for the soldier. Mr. Lincoln was a WINNER because of the way he treated "little people."

Jean Nabors, a graduate student in a university

class Dr. Leila Acklen and I taught, experienced the death of her twenty-six-year-old twin sister during the semester. At the beginning of the next class period she told us, "I learned that when you are gone, you are not remembered for things you have done for yourself but for things you have done for others." This advice, I hope, will motivate us toward a more "other-centered" philosophy. We've probably noticed many times that the happiest people are those who try to make WINNERS out of others. They realize that the greatest exercise in the world is reaching down and helping someone else up.

Perhaps you have heard of the group of researchers who set out to identify a common denominator among one hundred "self-made" millionaires. They wanted to share this profound research with the rest of the world. And what do you suppose they found in this group which varied in age from twenty-one to seventy, and whose educational backgrounds ranged from the third grade to Ph.D's? They found one common characteristic among the millionaires. They were all "goodfinders." They had the ability to find something good in every person and in every situation they encountered. The real WINNERS in life learned this attribute and developed the habit of practicing it. They weren't born with this trait. They practiced it, and practiced it, and practiced it until it became a habit, and their subconscious minds were programmed to look always for good things.

Why don't you get a sheet of paper and write down all the good things you can identify in some of the people you know? Then list some good things that have materialized because of some adverse experience you encountered. Practicing this simple technique will help you become a goodfinder—a WINNER.

In a motivation and personal growth class I was teaching one evening, a young school teacher told us how she had experienced beautiful serendipity as a result of a concern for an elderly lady. When she was in high school, her family lived across the street from an elderly lady who lived alone. Often she would take this lady out walking and sit with her in the park. Each week she would take her to the supermarket where the lady purchased her groceries.

Later, when the young lady was away attending college, she received a phone call to return home for the reading of the will of the elderly lady. Because the woman had lived primarily on social security, it was assumed that she had very little to bequeath. However, she had left her young friend property valued at $10,000.

My good friend from Texas, Herman Locke, taught me one of the most impressive lessons I've ever had. One day as we were stopping at a restaurant for dinner, we noticed a man staggering and falling against the building. Herman said, "That fellow must be drunk." We entered the restaurant and sat across from the man. After a few minutes Herman looked at me and said,

"Art, I owe someone an apology. That fellow over there isn't drunk. He's a double amputee and has to struggle just to get around." Although I'd always thought a great deal of Herman, since that day he has been a very special person to me. It takes a big person with a sensitive heart to apologize.

My favorite city to visit is San Francisco. My wife, Ann, and I love to ride the cable cars, visit Fisherman's Wharf, and eat at many of the city's famous restaurants. I am saddened at times to read of the people who have jumped off the Golden Gate Bridge to their deaths. Recently I read that over seven hundred people had jumped to their deaths. A couple of years ago one young man left this note in his apartment: "If, on the way to the Golden Gate Bridge, one person smiles at me, no one will ever find this suicide note." That morning this fellow needed a smile, and no one gave him one. Not one single person smiled at him! Question: "What if he had passed you?"

About seven one morning Eileen Burch telephoned and asked me, "Art, do you know what a smile is?"

I said, "No, what is a smile?"

She replied, "A smile is a gentle curve that straightens out many things."

Another friend sent me a description of a smile. I'm quoting it here, although I don't know its original source. It reads:

> A smile enriches those who receive, without making poorer those who give. It takes but a

moment, but the memory of it sometimes lasts forever. None is so rich or mighty that he can get along without it, none so poor but he can be made rich by it. A smile creates happiness in the home, fosters good will in business, and is the countersign of friendship. It brings rest to the weary, cheer to the discouraged, sunshine to the sad, and is nature's best antidote for trouble. Yet it cannot be borrowed or stolen, for it is something of no value to anyone unless it is given away. Some people are too tired to give you a smile. Give them one of yours, as none needs a smile so much as he who has no more to give.

There's a cute little story about a couple named Burton and Dorothy Jean Gooch that had been married for twenty-seven years and had never had an argument. That's right—twenty-seven years. Someone asked them how in the world they had managed to live together that long without having an argument. Dorothy Jean responded, "On our wedding night, we agree that Burton would always make the major decisions and I would make the minor ones. And to this day we have never had a major decision to make."

Although he may not always win, the WINNER knows that associating with other positive thinkers is good for him. It's like the farmer, Jack Roberts, from Knoxville, Tennessee, who entered his old horse in the Kentucky Derby. Jack said, "I know he doesn't stand much of a chance to win, but the association will be good for him."

WISDOM FROM WINNERS

WINNERS believe that a good attitude turns a chore into a cheer.

WINNERS know that how you think when you lose will determine how long it will be until you win.

WINNERS are convinced that you don't get a second chance to make a good first impression.

WINNERS believe that an optimist is a "happy-chondriac."

WINNERS believe that if you growl all day, you'll be dog-tired at night.

WINNERS know that a smile is so powerful it can even break ice.

WINNERS see a pessimist as one who feels bad when he feels good for fear he'll feel worse when he feels better.

ACTION SHEET
"The Most Important Thing About You"

Attitudes I Will Develop This Week

1.

2.

3.

4.

5.

ACTION SHEET
"The Most Important Thing About You"

Habits I Will Develop This Week

1.

2.

3.

4.

5.

ACTION SHEET
"The Most Important Thing About You"

Skills I Will Develop This Week

1.

2.

3.

4.

5.

ACTION SHEET
"The Most Important Thing About You"

The following list of people with a positive mental attitude are those with whom I will develop greater friendships this week:

1.

2.

3.

4.

5.

6.

7.

CHAPTER 2

The Secret Ingredient

"Readiness for opportunity makes for success. Opportunity often comes by accident; readiness never does."

SAM RAYBURN

One summer during my high school days I worked on a towboat which pushed barges of gasoline from Port Arthur, Texas, to Knoxville, Tennessee, to Paducah, Kentucky, and to Cairo, Illinois. This towboat, the *M.V. Codrington*, often sat for hours waiting for other barges and boats to go through the locks and dams on the beautiful Tennessee River. Although my mother and father never knew it, a friend and I would dive off the barges and swim in the cool water on those hot July days. If they had known this, I probably would have had the opportunity to work the rest of that summer at the service station in the small town where we lived. But I was tired of washing and greasing cars, repairing flats, and cleaning windshields. I wanted to see something other than what was under the hoods of cars and trucks. And I was thrilled my parents gave me permission to try something new and challenging.

Meanwhile, back to the barge where we were awaiting our turn to enter the lock . . . When the operator signaled for us to enter, our captain would blow the whistle for us to prepare the barges and towboat. The captain would maneuver the towboat and push the barges through the large steel doors that led into the lock. After we tied the barges, the operator would close the heavy doors and open the valves so the water could enter the lock and raise our barges. Sometimes it would take forty-five minutes for the water level to raise us to the dam. When we were level with this water, the other huge doors were opened, and we started up the Tennessee River again.

Sometimes our empty barges were hit with winds of eighty miles an hour. These winds kept our captain quite busy steering the towboat so that the cables holding the barges would not break and allow the barges to go where the river wanted them to go. Sometimes the water was so shallow that he slowed the engines so that our propellers would not hit the bottom and break. In other words, he adjusted the operating conditions to maximize our chances for a successful journey.

Sometimes the fog on the Mississippi was so dense that we had to tie the towboat and barges to the trees on the levee until the sun burned through the fog the next morning. But we never quit. We knew where we were going. Even when we had to dry-dock in New Orleans for repairs on the drive-shaft and propeller, we still didn't quit. We were on our way to a specific place.

Lock by lock we conquered the higher levels and mountains which stood between us and our destination. Armed with patience and persistence, our crew reached its destination. Our success in life can be favorably compared with our journey through the locks that raised us over the hills and dams. Too many people think that success in life is going to come in one big beautiful package.

Our big success is going to depend on our little successes as we sail through the channels of life. As the Chinese have told us for years, "A journey of a thousand miles begins with one step." And then, we might add, you must keep taking steps— one at a time.

Things seem to go smoothly at times in our lives. And then there are times when we have some rough sailing. Most of us don't go through life walking on mountain peaks. All of us must travel in the valley of frustration, anxiety, worry, stress, and despair. When you are experiencing these valleys, visualize those golden nuggets of self-fulfillment you enjoyed at the peaks of those previous mountain-top experiences. Remember that quite often it's down in the valley where the growth occurs. While you're in those valleys, ask yourself, "How can I use this experience creatively and constructively?" Your answer can help you be a WINNER. This world will be much better because you are a WINNER.

A WINNER is patient and realizes that be-
havioral and attitudinal changes often require
time for successful implementation. The beautiful pecan trees my father planted did not produce
pecans until long after he had planted them.
With patience and care he nurtured them into
large and productive trees. During the winter and
spring he fertilized them, and he spent time
watering them in the summer. Delicious pecans,
years later, were the result of his efforts.

During the spring each year my father would
use a horse or hire someone with a tractor to
break the ground for our family garden. Then
Dad would assign my brother, Tom, and me the
task of breaking all the large chunks of dirt with a
hoe. Because our hearts were at the basketball
court, we'd work as fast as we could to finish the
task. The next day Dad would take a hand plow
and till the rows for planting. Then Tom and
I would plant the seeds where he told us to. After
watering them, we'd run to the basketball court
again. We were motivated to play basketball,
while Dad was motivated to raise vegetables for
our family. He could visualize how those vegetables would look and taste in a few weeks.

Regardless of the preparation and work, I never
saw us plant squash seeds, potatoes, corn, or
other seeds one day and have those vegetables on
our table the next day. Several weeks later, after
we had watered the plants and hoed the grass
away, my sister, Annie Ruth, and Mother would
pick the vegetables and cook them for dinner or

can them to eat during the winter months. Those experiences taught us planning, patience, persistence, and cooperation.

My grandfather walked off and left my grandmother with five small children to raise. My father, who was in elementary school at the time, dropped out to take care of the cotton crop and provide food for the family. Although most people never knew it, my dad never returned to school to graduate. Perhaps a high school diploma wasn't as important or necessary in those days as it is today. Even though he didn't have a formal education, Dad could get along with anybody as well as handle his business matters appropriately. His human relations skills were so well developed that he could effectively interact with the mayor as well as the poorest citizen in town. People loved him throughout our small community. He was living proof of the saying that "when you don't have an education, you've got to use your brains."

In Las Vegas Floyd Johnston told me about a persistent lady who was determined to find a compatible husband. She married a rich oil man in Houston but divorced him after a year of marriage. Then she moved to Hollywood and married an actor who had starred in several movies. Six months later she divorced him. Then, of all things, she met a preacher in Kentucky and married him. She lived with him for three years before they were divorced. She moved to Florida and married an undertaker. Someone asked her why she had married all those fellows. She replied, "One for the money, two for the show, three to make ready, and four to go." That lady was really optimistic! Perhaps she was somewhat like the eighty-four-year-old fellow from Arkansas who married a twenty-two-year-old girl and bought a five-bedroom house next to an elementary school.

My wife and I spent a lovely week in Honolulu one summer when I was conducting a motivation and communication workshop. One afternoon we went out to swim and enjoy the sun and sand on beautiful Waikiki Beach. After we swam for a while, we sat on the beach visiting with some people we had met from Ohio. I noticed that a lady had come down to the beach with her two small children. She sat there while the children began walking toward the sea. They walked into the water just as a large wave came in. The wave knocked both boys off their feet. One of the little fellows jumped up laughing. The other boy was crying as he ran to his mother. The second reaction is the kind some people have when an adverse situation knocks them down. WINNERS believe that adverse situations in life make them better. Losers, on the other hand, become bitter.

One of the most rewarding experiences of my life happened one year when I directed a motivational and personal achievement program for a high school football team. I'll never forget one of the players named Rusty McClure. He was a hard-hitting, powerful fullback on offense, and he loved to play linebacker on defense. He didn't mind hitting or getting hit. He loved competition and winning. Early in the season Rusty's jaw was broken. A surgeon wired his jaw together and told him he was through playing football for the rest of the season. But the surgeon didn't know Rusty very well.

The next Friday evening I walked into the dressing room and saw Rusty dressed out and ready to play. I asked him what he was doing. He mumbled something and indicated that he was ready and eager to play football. Because his teeth were wired together, the only food he had had all week was liquid. He drank a lot of milk shakes during the month he was in this condition.

That night the coach allowed him to run with the ball on offense. As I recall, he gained about eighty yards in that game. When he came to the sidelines to rest for a few minutes, I felt sorry for him but was inspired as I watched him desperately trying to catch a breath of air with his teeth wired together. I can still see the agony on his face as he stood by me in that hot football uniform with the temperature hovering around ninety degrees. You can imagine how he inspired the other players with his desire and dedication.

The next Friday evening Rusty was dressed out and ready to play again. I could tell he had lost some weight. It had been fourteen days since he had eaten any solid food. Rusty played every play on offense that night. It was still hot and the humidity was high, but not as high as his desire to play and win. My heart ached as I watched him gasp for fresh air in the clouds of dust.

In the third week the coach allowed Rusty to play both offense and defense. This meant playing the entire game, and that's what Rusty wanted. He was still losing weight. For twenty-one days he had consumed liquids through a straw. He was still drinking those milk shakes. I sometimes wonder if he still likes milk shakes. But he made it that night on the field. It was thrilling to watch him cross the goal line with the football for a touchdown.

Rusty was really glad to see the next Friday evening. It was the last game he'd have to play with his wired jaw. He played well again that night as he gained more than one hundred yards running the football. Wouldn't a T-bone steak have looked good on his plate the next week?

At the end of the season a head football coach of a university called and asked me to write a letter of recommendation concerning Rusty and his potential. I wrote the coach that I had never seen a football player with the desire Rusty had.

WINNERS can take a *minus* and make a *plus* out of it. Their eyes are always open to creative opportunities for growth that negative situations can provide.

Failures provide WINNERS with opportunities to learn ways that do not work. As Charles Kettering said: "Every great improvement has come after repeated failures. Virtually nothing comes out right the first time. Failures, repeated failures, are fingerposts on the road to achievement."

Sometimes the WINNER realizes that he has to try another way in order to succeed. Jack Robertson, a paraplegic because of an automobile accident when he was nineteen years old, has been sitting in a wheelchair teaching students at an elementary school in Scottsdale, Arizona. At one time he had been an excellent swimmer. He decided that he wanted to be the first paraplegic to swim the English Channel. Jack spent two years developing, perfecting, and practicing a new free style windmill stroke.

Jack swam for eighteen hours in the English Channel before the tides forced him to be pulled from the water when he was within a few hundred yards from the shore. Back at the hotel in Folkestone, England, he declared, "I think I made my point. I have proved that such people as me can get off their backsides and do what we want to do."

WINNERS just don't give up easily. They have the tenacity to hang in tough. Like our son, Alan, who was the pitcher on a little league baseball team in Texas. Someone asked him what the score was. He replied, "It's 27-0."

"Well," said the adult, "I guess you all are really discouraged."

Alan looked at him and said, "No sir. Why should we be discouraged? We haven't gone to bat yet."

I love this exciting attitude. I'd want him on

my team if I were coaching another little league team again. He has a WINNER'S attitude.

WINNERS are inspired by the words of James J. Corbett:

> Fight one more round. When your feet are so tired that you have to shuffle back to the center of the ring, fight one more round. When your arms are so tired that you can hardly lift your hands to come on guard, fight one more round. When your nose is bleeding and your eyes are black and you are so tired that you wish your opponent would crack you on the jaw and put you to sleep, fight one more round—remembering that the man who always fights one more round is never whipped.

Theodore Roosevelt once observed, "Far better it is to dare mighty things, to win glorious triumphs, even though checkered by failure, than to take rank with those poor spirits who neither enjoy much nor suffer much, because they live in the gray twilight that knows not victory nor defeat." Roosevelt reminds us of the persistent attitude of that great inventor Thomas Edison. He said, "I never allow myself to become discouraged under any circumstances. The three great essentials to achieve anything worthwhile are: hard work, stick-to-itiveness, and common sense."

A real WINNER has the persistent attitude of one young lad who lived near Boston. Because he really needed a job, he began looking in the newspaper want ads every day. When he saw a job opening in Boston, he sat down and wrote the best letter he could and mailed it to P.O. Box 1935 in Boston. He carefully described his qualifications, interest in the job, and his willingness to work hard and learn. He waited nearly two weeks, but there was no response to his letter. He sat down and wrote a second letter and mailed it to P.O. Box 1935. Two more weeks passed and still there was no response.

This young man was not a quitter. He wrote a third letter describing his desire and determination to work for the company. He was disappointed when two more weeks passed and no word had come from the company. Probably ninety-five percent of our population would have felt they had gone the second mile and could justify quitting. But not this WINNER. He wanted that job badly enough to go a step further.

He boarded the train to Boston. He walked from the train station to the main post office. Upon entering the building, he inquired of the postmaster as to ownership of P.O. Box 1935. The postmaster informed him that it was against policy to release such information. Surely it was time to give up and look for some other job. No one would blame him now. But not this WINNER.

He walked around the post office for a while and came up with a beautiful idea. He located the box and stood over to the side, waiting. He waited for two hours, but no one came to get the mail from that box. Another two hours passed, and still no one came. Finally, toward the end of the day, a man arrived and collected the mail from the box. He followed the man for several blocks and into a large office building. When the man entered the elevator, he followed. The elevator stopped at the eleventh floor, and the man got off and walked into the office of a brokerage firm.

The young boy entered the office and asked the secretary if he might see the manager. The secretary was so impressed with the boy's pleasant attitude that she ushered him in. The boy introduced himself and told the manager that he had written three letters applying for the job the company had advertised, and that no one had responded to his letters. He told the manager he wanted to work so badly for the company that he had boarded a train to Boston, waited all day for someone to pick up the mail from P.O. Box 1935, and followed the man to this office. He then said, "And I'd like to have the job with your company. You'll be glad you hired me."

The manager was so impressed with the young man's attitude and persistence that he hired him. The young man started working as hard as he could to learn about the company and the details of his work. His attitude, persistence, and dedication resulted in a very successful career as a financial analyst. This WINNER'S name? Roger Babson.

Could you drive a car if you had no hands or arms? Would you be capable of typing without fingers? And could you tie a child's shoe strings if you were armless? Could you catch a fly in the air with your feet? It would take a very special person to accomplish these things, wouldn't it! Bonnie Consolo can do it! I've seen her engaged in these activities. It's almost one of those experiences which you have to see to believe.

Bonnie Consolo was born without arms. She was reared by two loving and caring parents on a small farm in Kentucky. She was one of five children and was the only one "handicapped." As a small girl she was given the responsibility of taking care of her baby brother while the rest of the family worked in the fields. That experience captured her heart and developed in her a burning desire to achieve a goal in life—to marry and have a family. She never lost sight of this goal and her burning desire moved her toward it.

In high school Bonnie learned how to type by using her toes. And she could type twenty-five words a minute! She also enjoyed her class in shorthand—or, as she called it, "shortfoot." Also, she took a class in driver education. She passed the driving test the first time she took it—and the car was a stick shift! When the girls played basketball, she usually kept the score. But guess who was chosen first when they played soccer?

After graduating from high school, Bonnie went to a rehabilitation center in Staunton, West Virginia because someone thought she needed to be rehabilitated. A few months later the occupational therapist called her into his office and asked, "Are you ready?"

She replied, "For what?"

He responded, "Your prosthesis."

She asked what that was and he told her it was artificial arms. She tried to refuse but he insisted that she learn how to use them. After a lot of training she finally mastered a few basic skills. But she could do all those things without those heavy, awkward, cumbersome arms! Why should she burden herself with them?

Bonnie left that center and moved to Florida where she worked as a PBX operator. While living there she found the best place for those "awkward arms" was in the closet! A newspaper reporter wrote a story about Bonnie's life and published it nationally. A gentleman named Frank Consolo, living in Redding, California read it and began writing her. After months of corresponding, she moved to California. Later they were married and are now the proud parents of two attractive sons, Mark and Matt.

This outstanding lady attributes so much of her success in life to her mother. When she was a small girl, her mother would require her to learn all the fundamental skills necessary to take care of one's self. When it took other children only a few seconds to button a button, sometimes it would take Bonnie several minutes. But her mother "made her do it." The same was true relative to dressing herself or tying shoes. Bonnie always knew her mother was available and would help her if she really needed it. Her mother laid the beautiful foundation for her to become the self-reliant person she is today.

Bonnie told me one day that a turning point came in her life when she was thirteen years old. She began to wonder why she had to be so different from the other girls in her school. She became depressed as she compared herself to others. Then one night things came together. She decided that God had put her on this earth for a particular mission. And that mission was to develop her talents and show others what one could do with a "limited" body. She could prove to the world that the most important thing is not what we have lost, but what we do with what we have left that really counts!

Believing that others would be inspired by her life, Bonnie portrayed her attitude and talents in a provocative and amazing film entitled, "A Day in the Life of Bonnie Consolo." If you haven't seen this film, you have missed a great one. The film has won numerous national awards. I've shown it to many audiences where I have given a motivational speech or conducted a workshop. Without exception, every group has been inspired by it. Also, Bonnie travels around the country speaking to various groups. I hope you have an opportunity to hear her personally.

Today, Bonnie and her family live in Westerville, Ohio. She enjoys cooking for and taking care of her family. That hits her hot button!

WINNERS *make* things happen. They don't

sit around waiting for something to happen to them. They are aggressive individuals who put energy into their desires and positive thoughts. They know that good things will happen in their lives as a result of the seeds they plant and the territory they cultivate.

The philosopher Kierkegaard often related the story about a flock of geese that headed south to avoid the cold winter snows. After a few days of flying, they landed on a farm and ate a great deal of corn. When the flock started to fly off the next morning, one goose decided to stay a little longer and enjoy the delicious free corn. He planned to leave the next morning, but the corn still looked good. He gave the same reason for staying the next several days. He fully intended to fly south soon.

His procrastination helped create a habit pattern. Then cold weather hit the area. The goose either had to fly south or freeze to death. He started running across the field to build up enough speed to fly, but he had one problem: he was too fat to fly. Procrastination cost him his life.

Winston Churchill's positive attitude and indomitable spirit during the dark days of World War II were reflected in the encouragement he gave the British people. He said, "Tomorrow will be better. The day will come when we will win. The final victory will be ours." After the war, Churchill was invited to speak to the boys enrolled in the school he had attended. The headmaster told the boys to bring notebooks and copy down everything their guest said, because they were to hear the greatest living Englishman. Churchill walked to the platform and looked at the faces of all those boys. He realized that life would hold many opportunities as well as challenges for them. His complete speech was simple: "Never give in, never give in, never give in, never, never, never, never!" He then sat down. These words are just as powerful and meaningful today as they were then.

One of the speeches I deliver throughout America contains three tremendously important points relative to personal and professional achievement. Here they are:

1. PERSISTENCE
2. PERSISTENCE
3. PERSISTENCE

A retired executive once stated that the secret of every successful businessman he had known lay in three little words: "and then some." The man who got ahead was the one who would do what he was assigned to do, and then some. He was the man who worked the hours required by his contract, and then some. He would treat the men under him fairly, and then some. This businessman was simply applying the Biblical principle of going "the second mile." This persistent attitude is a noticeable characteristic in all WINNERS.

Persistence is often the determining attitude that separates the WINNER from the loser. The

WINNER doesn't give in, doesn't give out, doesn't give over, and doesn't give up. He's somewhat like my friend Joe Villemez. Joe's nephew went to him for some important counseling. It seems that the boy had fallen in love and wanted to marry this beautiful girl, but he didn't have any money and couldn't find a job. Joe, the wise counselor, told the boy he had a solution to the problem. He had located a job for the boy in a city about fifteen hundred miles away. The boy responded, "But I can't go. She'll forget all about me while I'm over there for a year working to save money so that we can get married."

Joe said, "David, that's no problem. Just write her a long love letter every day, and she'll always be thinking about you." In desperation the boy decided to try it. And sure enough this concept of spaced repetition and persistence worked. When David returned home in a year, he found that his loved one had married the postman.

In my judgment, Calvin Coolidge gave us a most provocative insight into the concept of persistence. He said,

> Nothing in the world can take the place of persistence. Talent will not; nothing is more common than unsuccessful men with talent. Genius will not; unrewarded genius is almost a proverb. Education will not; the world is full of educated derelicts. Persistence and determination alone are omnipotent. The slogan 'Press on' has solved and always will solve the problems of the human race.

The Duke of Wellington said that the British soldiers at the Battle of Waterloo were not any braver than Napoleon's soldiers, but they were braver for five minutes longer.

The WINNER develops persistence in all his pursuits. He reflects the attitude toward life of the man who built a successful business on the philosophy that "it's always too soon to quit."

A WINNER doesn't sell himself short. He continues striving, pushing, and tugging to achieve his objectives. You've probably read or seen copies of the famous children's books written by Dr. Seuss (actually Theodore Geisel). The first book he wrote was rejected by twenty-seven publishers. They critiqued his manuscript and concluded that it contained too much fantasy and verse. Theodore Geisel believed in the book. He believed in his writing ability. He was persistent. And because of his persistence the *twenty-eighth* publisher liked the unusual approach Geisel had taken in his writing. The company bought it. Millions of books by this writer have since been sold. The next time you try something and don't succeed, ask yourself, "Have I tried twenty-eight times?" WINNERS sometimes have to.

WISDOM FROM WINNERS

WINNERS believe that failure is the path of least persistence.

WINNERS don't make tomorrow's meal with yesterday's garbage.

WINNERS say, "Patience is keeping your motor in neutral when you feel like stripping the gears."

WINNERS get ahead because they do more than is expected . . . and keep on doing it.

WINNERS know there is no such thing as failure—only new beginnings.

WINNERS believe that success is that point in life where preparation and opportunity meet; but a great number of people don't recognize it because it comes disguised as hard work.

WINNERS are aware that procrastination is the grave in which opportunity is buried.

ACTION SHEET
"The Secret Ingredient"

This week I will be persistent in the following pursuits:

1.

2.

3.

4.

5.

CHAPTER 3

Keeping Your
Hot Button Hot

*"Nothing worthwhile was ever accomplished
without the will to start, the enthusiasm to
continue, and the persistence to complete."*

WAITE PHILLIPS

Someone has said that there are four kinds of people in America. *First*, there are those who *make* things happen. These individuals have a positive attitude about themselves, others, their jobs, families, and America. They are the builders who believe that life is worth living. When they fall down, they get up and get on with the business of living. They realize that how you think when you lose will determine how long it will be until you win again. They know that a good attitude turns a chore into a cheer.

These people who make things happen agree with the words of wisdom from W. Clement Stone, founder of the Combined Insurance Company: "One's attitude is the only thing over which he has absolute, complete control." These WINNERS are the ones who turn stumbling blocks into steppingstones. They see things and situations from creative, constructive viewpoints.

Second, there are those people who *watch* things happen. They are in the group that is neither for nor against apathy. They don't oppose those who are involved in creative and productive activities. For reasons of their own they choose not to become involved in the exciting adventure of attempting new experiences. In far too many cases this feeling is projected because the person fears failure. This fear of failure is probably, of all obstacles, the greatest deterrent to growth and achievement in a person's life. He fears that if he tries something and it fails, people will look with disfavor or pity on him, and that a parent, spouse, or friend will say, "I told you that wouldn't work!" And then he'll feel guilty as a result.

Where would America be today if scientists and technologists had refused to dream, attempt, or experiment because they might have failed? We wouldn't be reading by electric light bulbs, listening to the radio, riding in airplanes, driving cars, and seeing the significant reduction in diseases such as polio. WINNERS win because they believe that victory is possible any time they're active in improving themselves and trying to improve this world for others.

Third, there are those who simply *wonder* what has happened. Periodically, they wake up to see the results of something that has happened and wonder, "What in the world has happened?"

They are probably not happy with themselves and wonder "how others always get the lucky breaks."

A WINNER worries, but not very much. He knows that worry is a counter-productive emotion. He is aware that worrying is holding onto a mental picture of what he doesn't want to happen. It's like the fellow who was sentenced to die in the electric chair. His lawyer kept telling him not to worry; everything was going to be okay. One day the prison officials came to get the condemned man. As they were walking to the electric chair, he asked the guards if he could make one last telephone call. The guards agreed. He telephoned his lawyer and complained, "I thought you told me not to worry. I'm on my way to the electric chair. What advice do you have to give me?"

The lawyer replied, "My best advice is: don't sit down."

Fourth, there are those who usually *criticize* what has happened. These folks are born in the objective case and stay in the kickative mood. Their eyes are always open for opportunities—opportunities to criticize others. They refuse to participate in constructive activities. They belong to the group which follows this adage: "Why be disagreeable when, with a little effort, you can be a real stinker!" And you'll notice that most people avoid spending much time with members of this negative club.

There isn't a single person in this world who

can make us think negatively, unless we allow him to. We control our thinking. If someone else influences us to think negatively, it only shows that we have given him permission to make us think that way. Our bosses, parents, children, spouses, friends, enemies, co-workers, and anyone else can program us to think negatively only if we allow them to.

Recently, when I was fulfilling a speaking engagement, I had the privilege of sharing the platform in Moline, Illinois with the writer, Sidney Harris. In visiting with him prior to the time we were to speak, I asked him about a lovely editorial he had written some years before. The editorial had been about his walking with a friend to a newsstand where his friend purchased a newspaper every day. When they arrived at the newsstand, Sidney's friend warmly greeted the owner and politely asked for a newspaper. The owner rudely shoved the paper at him, complained that the man didn't have the correct change, and directed more verbal abuse at him. On the way home Sidney asked him if he purchased a newspaper there every day.

"Yes, I do," he replied.

"And does he always treat you that way?" Sidney asked.

"Well, I must tell you that he does," his friend replied.

Sidney then said, "Why don't you buy a newspaper somewhere else?"

His friend then offered this fantastic response:

"I refuse to let him dictate how I am going to act."

What beautiful advice! WINNERS are positive and enthusiastic regardless of the way others around them act.

Dr. John O'Brien, research professor of theology at the University of Notre Dame, says the word "enthusiasm" comes from two Greek words, *theos* and *entae*, which mean "God within you." Isn't this a beautiful concept? God wants you to be a WINNER. As Ethel Waters said, "God doesn't sponsor any flops." God feeds the birds, but they have to go and get the seeds.

An exciting Texan I know, Larry McKenzie, defines enthusiasm as "inner excitement." That is the best definition I've heard. It suggests that enthusiasm isn't necessarily shown by loud talking, backslapping, or other external behavior. In fact, genuine enthusiasm must fit one's personality to be effective. For example, Dr. Jonas Salk was filled with enthusiasm, or inner excitement, as he quietly worked in his research laboratory discovering the polio vaccine.

The Bible says that with faith we can move mountains. I believe it. God didn't say the mountains would be moved immediately. But they will be moved! Think of yourself as a co-worker with God. Each day you're praying for His will to be done in your life. You and God are a majority. That's why I love to repeat each morning those exciting words from Psalms 118:24: "This is the day the Lord has made; we will rejoice and be glad in it."

While I was a post-doctoral fellow at the University of Southern California School of Medicine, I was impressed by a plaque I saw in a building on the main campus. It contained the words of Waite Phillips: "Nothing worthwhile was ever accomplished without the will to start, the enthusiasm to continue, and the persistence to complete."

The epitaph for too many people could read: "Died at 43. Buried at 67." It's obvious that these people reduced their efforts for growth and excitement when they were forty-three years old. These are the ones who need to be reminded of all those people who achieved their goals in life after the age of forty.

Recently I was delivering a speech in the lovely MacDonald Hotel in Edmonton, Alberta. After the presentation some members of the planning committee invited me to lunch. One of the fellows knew that I collected ideas for my speeches. After lunch he gave me a copy of a book entitled *How to Succeed Without Working*. Now, that title sounds fascinating. In bold print on the first page was the word IMPOSSIBLE. The rest of the "book" contained blank pages on which to take notes.

You've noticed that WINNERS have a sense of humor. They can laugh at themselves and also laugh *with* others and not at them. They're like the fellow named Hal Walker, who applied for a job as a vice-president of a large company in Marked Tree, Arkansas. The owner decided to ask him some questions to test his ability to make important decisions. He said, "Hal, if you were standing down by the train station and saw two trains coming toward each other on the same track at forty miles an hour, what would you do?

After thinking for a moment, Hal responded, "I'd go home and get my brother."

"What?" the owner asked. "You'd go get your brother? Why in the world would you do that?"

"Because he ain't never seen a train wreck before," Hal responded.

WINNERS are not spectators in the game of life. They are active participants in this exciting adventure. They refuse to sit on the sidelines and watch things happen. They want to make things happen. They're not like those timid souls who are afraid to participate because they might be rejected by someone, or they might get hurt, or they might fail. Mother used to tell us that old Uncle Hank was always going to do something, and he finally did. He died.

The WINNER knows that life is a real game in which every day is the Super Bowl. But he knows that it's much more important than that professional football contest. For example, there are no "time outs" during which the clock of life is stopped. It keeps moving—all the time. Also, there are no substitutions in the game of life. You have to play your own position. No one can substitute for you—no one. Your success depends on what you can get out of *you*. Not what any coach, boss, spouse, or parent can get out of you, but what you can.

Life is not a scrimmage either. It's the real thing.

When I played football, the coach had us run a particular play. Then he would stop, critique the play, and we'd run it again. And sometimes we'd run it again, and again, and again. Life doesn't provide us these options. None of us can relive any single day, regardless of its successes or failures. After twenty-four hours, that day is gone forever. That's why it's such a fantastic idea to awaken each morning and get up with enthusiasm on the right side of the mind.

Arnold Toynbee once stated, "Apathy can only be overcome by enthusiasm, and enthusiasm can only be aroused by two things: first, an ideal that takes the imagination by storm; second, a definite intelligible plan for carrying that ideal into practice." This idea indicates that we need to set a goal that we simply must reach, then build the fire of a burning desire under it. Enthusiasm is an attribute which can be developed by thinking about a worthwhile goal until it obsesses you. Enthusiasm will propel you to achieve those goals. George Matthew Adams once suggested, "Enthusiasm is a kind of faith that has been set fire."

Enthusiasm is as contagious as measles and as powerful as dynamite. It can move mountains of apathy and increase production to undreamed of heights. Enthusiasm is to the WINNER what rocket fuel is in the cylinders that launch our astronauts into space. It creates motion. It causes things to happen.

Last summer a boy from New York City was hiking at night in the Rocky Mountain National

Park. He asked Alan Hewitt, the guide, "Is it true that a grizzly bear won't attack you if you're carrying a flashlight?"

"That depends," the guide answered, "on how fast you're carrying it."

Some folks are turned on to activities which really excite them. They remind us of the question: "Does success come before enthusiasm, or does enthusiasm come before success? In my judgment, enthusiasm comes before success. It's the driving force that helps a WINNER achieve his goals.

Positive desire and negative fear are the two strongest psychological forces within the human being. Desire is not something that can be measured by a standardized achievement test. In my judgment, it is the strongest force, and it can move people to achieve seemingly unattainable goals. WINNERS have a strong desire to achieve. They think, plan, talk, and act with an "I can" attitude. They pay the price to win.

Someone asked Frederick Williamson, a former president of the New York Central Railway, his definition of success. He offered this:

> The longer I live, the more certain I am that enthusiasm is the little recognized secret of success. The difference in actual skill and ability and intelligence, between those who succeed and those who fail, is usually neither wide nor striking. But if two workers are nearly equally matched, the one who is enthusiastic will find the scales tipped in his or her favor. And the one of second-rate ability with enthusiasm will often

outstrip one of first-rate ability without enthusiasm.

Don't you just love to be around optimistic people? There was an old man in Ohio named Tharon Lee who was in his last days. The family was called to the hospital for the final hours. The family doctor was called to examine the old gentleman and give his prognosis. No member of the family was willing to tell the old fellow how much his condition had deteriorated; so the doctor leaned over to tell the old gentleman he had only a short while left and to ask if there were a final request. In a whisper the old fellow answered, "Yes, get me another doctor."

Harry Truman once said, "I have studied the lives of great men and women; and I found that the men and women who got to the top were those who did the jobs they had in hand, with everything they had of energy and enthusiasm and hard work."

Ask yourself: How would an enthusiastic person perform the work I am doing? Perhaps you'd like to write some things down and then review them each week for a month. As you implement these "energizers," you'll soon discover that it's more fun to go to work each day.

The WINNER isn't always the individual who has the most, but he is always the one who gives the most. He knows that it's when we've given more than we're asked that we have given our best. George Bernard Shaw said, "I don't believe in circumstances. The people who get on in this world are the people who get up and look for circumstances they want, and, if they can't find them, make them." The individual with enthusiasm will sometimes experience temporary defeat; but this doesn't stop him, because his enthusiasm lifts him up and keeps him going.

Sometimes even WINNERS find it a challenge to please everyone. Perhaps you've felt at times like the cab driver who was working in Los Angeles for a company that had acquired a reputation for being late in responding to telephone calls. The president of the company admonished the drivers to resolve the problems by responding more rapidly to the calls.

The next day Tony, one of the drivers, was cruising down the street when a lady called for a taxi. The radio dispatcher relayed the message immediately to all the cab drivers. Tony realized that he was directly in front of the lady's house. He quickly stopped his cab, walked briskly to the door, and rang the doorbell just moments after the lady had completed the call. She came to the door and he announced, "Lady, you called for a cab. I'm your driver, Tony."

The surprised lady looked at him and said, "Young man, I'm not going to ride with anyone who drives as fast as you."

WISDOM FROM WINNERS

WINNERS believe that it isn't the load that weighs us down; it's the way we carry it.

WINNERS believe that most folks don't really fail; they just quit trying.

WINNERS know that failure will never overtake them if they have a burning desire to succeed.

WINNERS are convinced that the best place to look for a helping hand is at the end of their arm.

WINNERS believe it is not how much we have, but how much we enjoy that brings happiness.

WINNERS look for the best in others because doing so brings out the best in themselves.

ACTION SHEET
"Keeping Your Hot Button Hot"

In order to experience a more productive and rewarding week, I am enthusiastically going to give more than is expected of me in the following ways:

1. Employment

2. Family

3. Religion

4. Community

ACTION SHEET
"Keeping Your Hot Button Hot"

*This week I will conquer the thief of enthusiasm
—procrastination—by taking action on:*

1.

2.

3.

4.

5.

ACTION SHEET
"Keeping Your Hot Button Hot"

I will also conquer the second thief of enthusiasm—indecision—by making decisions on the following matters:

1.

2.

3.

4.

5.

ACTION SHEET
"Keeping Your Hot Button Hot"

To conquer the third thief of enthusiasm—an unorganized day—I am going to accomplish these six things tomorrow in the order of their importance:

1.

2.

3.

4.

5.

6.

CHAPTER 4

Mirror, Mirror On the Wall

"It is when we've given more than we're asked that we have given our best."

A wise old man lived in a cave a few miles from a village. People from the village often went to the old man for advice and counseling. They found that his answers were always correct. Two boys decided one day that they were going to trick the old man. Their plan included catching a bird and having one of them hold the bird in his hand. They planned to approach the old man and ask, "Is the bird I hold in my hand alive, or is it dead?" If the old man answered "Alive," the boy was to quickly squeeze the little bird in his hand and kill it. He would then open his hand and prove the old man wrong. If, however, the old man said, "The bird is dead," the boy would open his hand and show him that the bird was alive.

The boys walked out to the old man's cave. One of the boys said, "Old man, is the bird I hold in my hand alive, or is it dead?" The old man thought for a few moments and responded, "That depends on you. Its life is in your hands."

The WINNER realizes that *his* life is primarily in his hands. He can choose to use it or abuse it; mend it or break it; be somebody or nobody, an asset or a liability.

You can select your own epitaph today. WINNERS know their epitaphs. They live every day to epitomize them. I told my wife I want this epitaph on my tombstone: "He died learning."

Every day I try to do something to improve my mind. I may read a book, listen to a cassette tape, hear some motivational speaker, do research in a library, watch some informative or inspirational program on television, or visit with someone to discuss something. Just as I exercise and watch my diet to care for my body, I feel it is important to do something to improve my mind. I believe *you* think the same way. That's why you are reading this book.

After visiting the Alps someone related the story of the monument he had seen to a famous mountain climber who had died while trying to climb a dangerous pass. The epitaph on his tombstone read: "He died climbing." What a powerful thought. Like most of us, you're probably not terribly excited about being rushed to the cemetery in a casket. WINNERS know, however, that they're writing chapters each day in their lives, and they want the chapters to be productive.

A farmer in Kankakee, Illinois advertised for someone to work on his farm. After running the ad in the paper for three weeks, he finally received a phone call about the job. He invited the eighteen-year-old boy out for an interview. After showing him around the farm, he asked the young fellow, "Can you drive a tractor?"

"No sir," the boy replied.

"Well, can you operate a milking machine?" the farmer asked.

The boy responded, "No sir. I've never done that either."

The farmer asked several more questions and received negative answers to each one.

The farmer was growing short in patience and asked, "Well, what *can* you do?"

The young fellow said, "I can sleep when the wind blows."

The farmer didn't understand what he meant, but he needed help so badly that he gave the boy the job. A few days later a storm came up in the middle of the night. The wind was blowing about fifty miles an hour, accompanied by thunder, lightning, and rain. The farmer awoke and ran to the barn to check on the animals and the equipment.

He went to the room where the boy was sleeping soundly. Rather than trying to awaken the youth, the farmer ran out to check on the animals and equipment. He found the barn doors securely fastened. The animals were in their shelters and secured. Then he remembered a hay pile that was surely blowing away, but he found it covered well with canvas. On the way back to the house the farmer remembered what the boy had said: "I can sleep when the wind blows." And he understood.

This story reflects an attitude of pride. Pride in oneself and in one's work. It also speaks to the important work ethic that was much stronger in the past than it appears to be in our country today. A better world really does begin with *me*. The WINNER knows that he can change his world. He makes things happen by taking positive action.

The WINNER believes that the greatest freedom in the world is the freedom to become the best he is capable of becoming. He accepts the profound truth expressed by Ralph Waldo Emerson, "What lies behind us and what lies before us are tiny matters compared to what lies within us." Indeed, your success depends on what you can get out of *you*.

A friend recently told me about a tramp who was sitting on a park bench. As he watched a fellow walk by in a three-piece suit—obviously a successful person, the man said, "There, except for me, go I." This provocative statement characterizes the lives of many people. It seems that a lot of folks these days are itching for things they're not willing to scratch for.

Have you noticed how many people quit looking for work as soon as they find a job? Last December I went into a shoe store to buy a pair of shoes. The manager was standing by the door and I asked him, "How many people work here?"

He replied, "About half."

Some ten minutes later a salesman came to assist me. I asked him, "How long have you been working here?"

He said, "Ever since they threatened to fire me."

We have two chances of making good without working: slim and none.

A friend once told me about a young boy who went into a grocery store and asked permission to use the telephone. He called and asked to speak to Dr. Walter Murphy. He asked, "Do you need someone to mow your yard and clean the flower beds?" Dr. Murphy told him that he didn't because he already had a boy working for him. The boy asked if the worker did a good job and was dependable. Dr. Murphy assured him that the boy did excellent work. He thanked the doctor and hung up the receiver.

As the boy was leaving the grocery store, the manager, who was impressed with the boy's attitude, told him that he had a job opening and could use him. The boy responded, "Thank you, sir, but I already have a job. I'm Dr. Murphy's boy. I was just checking up on myself."

In my judgment, it's a good policy to watch the person in front of the one behind you.

As the popular motivational speaker Zig Ziglar says in his bestselling book *See You at the Top*, "Get rid of that stinking-thinking," and what we need is a "check-up from the neck-up." Zig places the responsibility for personal growth and achievement directly on our own shoulders. And that's where it should be.

Is there a common denominator among the personal traits of WINNERS? Yes. It is the capacity to make yourself do what needs to be done, whenever it needs to be done, whether you like it or not.

A few years ago a young man graduated from Arlington Heights High School in Fort Worth, Texas. He completed his freshman year of college at Texas Tech and went back to the Fort Worth area to find summer employment. Since he had enjoyed singing so much, he auditioned for a job at the amusement park, "Six Flags Over Texas." At the conclusion of the audition, he was told that he wasn't good enough to be a singer. Although disappointed, he did not give up. He spent the summer working as an operator helping people on and off rides at "Six Flags." This positive attitude and persistence paid off very well for John Denver. He believed in himself. He reflected the beautiful truth expressed by Eleanor Roosevelt, "Nobody can make you feel inferior without your permission."

WINNERS realize that it is impossible to please everyone. Tommy and Liz Lane were traveling in their car on their honeymoon. Before they arrived at the motel, the new bride said to her husband, "Please don't tell anyone that we're newlyweds because they'll laugh and make jokes about us."

When they entered the lobby to register, she stood back while he signed the directory. After spending the night there, they came back to the lobby area to pay for their lodging. She stood in the middle of the lobby while he paid the bill. As she stood there, other guests were frowning at her from her head to foot. She thought to herself, "I know he told them we are newlyweds. Just look at the expressions on their faces. I'll tell him off when we get in the car."

As they were driving off, Liz said, "Now tell me the truth. You told them we were just married, didn't you?"

He looked at her and said, "No, I didn't tell them we were newlyweds. I told them we were just good friends."

Sam Rayburn once said, "Readiness for opportunity makes for success. Opportunity often comes by accident. Readiness never does."

The measure of our success is not dependent on how much talent we have, but on how much we use it. Research tells us that nine-tenths of an iceberg is below water. Could it be that nine-tenths of your potential is out of sight—just waiting to be developed and used?

A WINNER is aware that his success begins with himself, and that no success principle will work unless *he* does.

WINNERS believe that with God's help they can do anything they really want to do. They believe in the passage recorded in Philippians 4:13, "I can do all things through Him who

strengthens me." God made each of us a WIN-
NER. God loves WINNERS. And we are WIN-
NERS when we are developing the talents God
has given us and contributing each day toward
making this world a more beautiful place in
which to live.

Frank Vander Maaten lived in Sioux County,
Iowa. The citizens were filled with pride because
of his unusual ability to play the violin. As a
matter of fact, they expected him to become
world famous. At the age of eighteen, he was
working one day in his father's blacksmith shop.
Accidentally, a red-hot iron fell on his left hand,
burning him badly. The burn was so severe that
only his thumb and four stubs remained on the
hand. This was the hand he used to touch the
violin strings.

Such an accident would seem to be a justifiable
reason to put the violin in the closet permanently.
And that's what everybody thought Frank would
do. But that thought wasn't on the mind of this
WINNER. This accident provided another opportunity for him—an opportunity to learn to
play the violin with his other hand. This stumbling block became a stepping-stone. Frank
learned to hold the bow in his crippled hand and
manipulate the strings with his good hand. It is to
his credit that he later became a noted violinist in
the Sioux City Symphony. WINNERS turn circumstances to their advantage—to help themselves and others.

A WINNER believes it is absolutely imperative

to have a healthy attitude about himself. If you don't like yourself, then who will? How we see ourselves is our ego. How other people see us is our personality. A healthy attitude toward ourselves suggests a confident pride in ourselves and our abilities. It's a belief and knowledge that we can achieve our goals. This does not suggest an ego trip in which one is all wrapped up in himself. Such a trip is of short duration. We don't want to be like the fellow who wrote a book entitled *The Four Most Beautiful People in the World, and How I Met the Other Three.*

Thomas Edison was asked by a young news reporter at a press conference, "Mr. Edison, how does it feel to have failed 10,000 times on this project?"

Edison looked at him for a moment, smiled, and said, "Young man, I did not fail 10,000 times. I simply found 10,000 ways that would not work."

This persistent attitude resulted in 1,093 inventions. Edison believed in himself. Although WINNERS don't always succeed at every task they attempt, they refuse to allow other people's opinions to kill their beliefs in themselves.

In her book *Think Mink*, Mary Crowley offers ten two-letter words to help make WINNERS out of those associated with her in the business she founded and has led to a sales volume of $100 million a year. Her advice: "If it is to be, it is up to me."

The measure of a WINNER is the size of the thing it takes to get him down. Show me a person who lets failure and defeat teach him wisdom, and I'll show you a WINNER. There is really no such thing as failure, only new beginnings. How we think when we lose will determine how long it will be until we win. As Dr. Alfred Adler has written, "One of the wonder-filled characteristics of human beings is their power to turn a minus into a plus."

Congratulations if you have failed and learned something helpful from your failure. Every inventor, musician, artist, athlete, scholar, scientist, and teacher has known failure. No one starts out a self-actualized person. Every person at some place and time failed to achieve his objectives or goals. Thomas Edison, Henry Ford, Jonas Salk, Franklin Roosevelt, and Michael DeBakey failed as they were learning, experimenting, and growing. I characterize these men as successful failures. They had deep beliefs in themselves. Their work has benefited millions of people. What if they had given up too soon?

WISDOM FROM WINNERS

WINNERS are those who can give without remembering and take without forgetting.

WINNERS firmly believe that the road to success
is always under construction.

WINNERS grow happiness under their feet, while
losers look for it in the distance.

WINNERS believe that the world owes them a
living, but they have to work to collect it.

WINNERS find an opportunity in every difficulty. Losers find a difficulty in every opportunity.

WINNERS believe past experiences should be a
guidepost—not a hitching post.

WINNERS view obstacles as opportunities to
develop their achievement muscles.

ACTION SHEET
"Mirror, Mirror on the Wall"

The following list reflects my major strengths and assets: (Please include attitudes, skills, traits, emotional and physical characteristics, education, and personality traits.)

1.

2.

3.

4.

5.

6.

7.

8.

9.

10.

11.

12.

13.

14.

15.

ACTION SHEET
"Mirror, Mirror on the Wall'

The following written description portrays the mental picture I have of myself succeeding:

ACTION SHEET
"Mirror, Mirror on the Wall"

This week I learned these new things that improved my knowledge of my job:

1.

2.

3.

4.

5.

ACTION SHEET
"Mirror, Mirror on the Wall"

Each day this week I am going to look in a mirror and give myself the following pep talk:

CHAPTER 5

What You Set
Is What You Get

*Belief is the thermostat that regulates our
accomplishments.*

Recently I boarded a plane for a trip to San
Francisco, where I was scheduled to conduct a
three-day seminar. After we were seated, the pilot
spoke over the public address system: "Good
morning, ladies and gentlemen. This is Captain
Turner. Welcome aboard Flight 241, non-stop to
San Francisco. Our cruising altitude will be
thirty-four thousand feet. We plan to arrive on
schedule at 2:43 P.M. The weather is nice in San
Francisco, with sunny skies and a temperature of
seventy-five degrees. Please sit back and enjoy
your flight. If any of our crew can assist you,
please call on us."

Now, I like that kind of introduction to my
flights. The pilot knew where he was going, what
the departure and arrival times were, and what
some of the conditions would be along the way.

How do you think I would have felt if the pilot

had greeted us with these words: "Welcome aboard, ladies and gentlemen. We will depart sometime this morning on a trip to San Francisco. We'll leave Memphis International Airport and fly south for a while; we'll probably fly west for an hour or two, and then we'll probably turn north for a while. We haven't decided on the particular cruising altitude yet, but we'll try to keep the aircraft above the mountain peaks. We don't know the weather conditions in San Francisco. We're not sure what time we will arrive, but we can assure you we'll have a lot of fun on this flight."

How long would you stay on that plane?

This fabricated captain's speech reminds me of the cross-eyed javelin thrower. He didn't win many contests, but he surely kept the spectators alert and interested.

Our goals will have a great deal more power when we make them personal, state them specifically, write them down, have them compatible with our values, state them positively, and make them challenging enough to motivate us to attain them.

Goals are the key to success. If a person doesn't have any goals, he won't know when he scores. I am reminded of two basketball teams lining up for the tip-off. Before the referee blows the whistle to begin the game, two men bring out a ladder and remove both goals. The referee then says, "Let's play ball!" How can the fellows play basketball if there are no goals? Who will know when someone scores? Who would enjoy this kind of a game? This is analogous to a person's not having specific goals for his life.

There is a powerful proverb which states, "Before you can score, you must have a goal." Exactly how much money do you want to earn next year? How many books do you plan to read this month? What kind of house do you want to own? How much time do you want to invest in service to your community? What kind of person do you want to be spiritually? How much do you want to weigh in six months? What particular skills do you plan to develop or improve in the next twelve months?

It is imperative that we define the target for which we are shooting, or we will never know how close we come to hitting it. We must define the height we want to reach, or we'll have no way of knowing when or if we've reached it. Without goals there is no way we can measure our success and achievement.

Goals help us build self-confidence. Because self-confidence is built upon successful experiences, setting and reaching goals enhances this attribute. In the goal-setting workshops I conduct, I often suggest that participants may want to begin by writing simple, achievable goals. For example: to read one specific book this week, or bake a cake for someone, or sign up for some exercise program, or write two letters in the morning, or call on three new prospective clients.

Several years ago there was a popular play on

Broadway. It ended with this powerful benediction, "May your dreams be your only boundaries." This is a phenomenal prescription to take every day. Before you retire at night, when you awaken each morning, and during the day, "dream your impossible dream." Each of us is limited only by the boundaries of our imagination. It is important to raise our sights above those things around us and catch a higher vision of the things we want to do with our lives. We'll find this advice in the Bible: "Look up! Set your mind on things that are above, not on things that are on the earth."

If we spend an inordinate amount of time on things around us, we may become quite discouraged. This dissipates our ability to dream and reach out toward important goals.

My favorite sport in high school was basketball. For three years my brother and I played on the varsity team. Because I played the guard position, it was my responsibility to bring the ball up the court. I developed the habit of looking down as I dribbled the basketball. It was impossible for me to see where the other players were positioned on the court when I had my head down. During practice sessions Coach Calvin Hastings would yell, "Art, look up!" With his encouragement and instruction, I broke that habit. When our son, Alan, played basketball, I noticed that he dribbled with his head up so that he had a clearer view of where he was going and where his teammates were.

You probably remember the lesson Jesus taught

Peter about walking on the water. Jesus told Peter to walk toward him on the water. Peter was progressing well on top of the water as long as he kept his eyes on Jesus. When Peter looked down at his feet, he saw the waves, became frightened, and began to sink.

One of the greatest lessons I have learned in life is that of the self-fulfilling prophecy. This concept clearly suggests that we become what we imagine; that we become what we *expect* to become. While we vividly picture ourselves achieving our goals, we will move toward their achievement. As Napoleon Hill stated, "What the mind can conceive and believe, it can achieve."

Psychologists tell us that we move in the direction of our present dominant thoughts. This is why it is essential to fill our minds with goal-oriented thoughts. This process nourishes one's subconscious mind with the proper mental food. The subconscious mind operates much like an automatic guidance system of a modern missile. It receives a set of planned instructions, monitors the course of the flight, and makes appropriate corrections to remain on course.

Without goals our minds wander aimlessly. Probably ninety-five percent of the adults who inhabit spaceship earth have no specific goals for their lives. This means they function like ships without rudders.

One summer while I was working on a towboat, we were pushing several barges of gasoline up the Mississippi River. The boat hit some heavy object under the water and the rudder was broken. We were adrift—unable to control our direction. The towboat and barges turned wildly as we helplessly floated downstream. Our captain finally made radio contact with another towboat, and it came to our rescue.

You can decide today—right now—that you are not going to drift aimlessly any longer. You are going to join the elite five percent who set goals and, as a result, achieve much more in life than do those without goals. One of the exciting things about living is that it is never too late to set specific goals for our lives.

All human progress was first visualized in someone's mind. This is true in business, education, medicine, engineering—in all endeavors. Christopher Columbus cherished a vision of a water route to the Indies, but discovered, instead, a "new world." Henry Ford dreamed of mass production of automobiles. Thomas Edison dreamed of inventing a technique to illuminate homes and offices in America. Dr. Jonas Salk cherished a vision of developing a vaccine against the dreaded polio. They all proved this point: to actualize, you must visualize.

A burning desire is often more important than knowledge. A study of the life of Thomas Edison reveals that he had little formal training in chemistry, mathematics, physics, or electronics—subjects ordinarily considered essential for an inventor. This great inventor, who obtained 1,093 patents, had a burning desire which could not be extinguished by discouragement or lack of adequate resources. He was willing to pay any price to achieve his goals.

Guidelines for Setting Goals

Decide specifically what you want to achieve in life.

WINNERS know what they want in order to achieve it. As Will Rogers said, "In order to succeed, you must know what you are doing, like what you are doing, and believe in what you are doing." The things you achieve by reaching your goals are not nearly as important as what you become by reaching them.

I suspect that when most of us look back over our lives, we'll be somewhat like the fellow, Amakel. One afternoon he was riding his camel in a caravan with a group of merchants who were traveling to a distant city to sell their merchandise. A voice out of the sky spoke to Amakel and said, "Get on your camel and ride by yourself to an oasis ten miles west of here. When the stars come out tonight, pick up all the pebbles you see by the oasis and put them in your pockets. And in the morning you will be both glad and sad."

Amakel did as he was instructed. After he had picked up several pebbles, he became tired and went to sleep. He awoke several times during the night wondering what the voice meant about feeling glad and sad. When the sun warmed his face, he rubbed his eyes and stood up to stretch. He reached into his pockets and pulled out the pebbles he had placed there. When he looked in his hand, he knew then what the voice meant. The pebbles had turned into jewels. He was glad he had picked up many of them but sad he had not picked up more.

You have the power TODAY to decide on the number and quality of "pebbles" you want to pick up. It's a very important decision for you to make. I want you to make the decision to do with your life what you really want to do. I wrote this book to help you become a greater WINNER. God wants you to be a WINNER. He created you and has given you talents to develop. Your love for God will be shown by what you do with those talents. Also, I hope you're making a great deal of money, because I believe the more money you're making, the more people you are serving.

Here are some examples of specific goals you might set: "Within two years I intend to be a district sales manager, or earn $50,000 a year, or complete my college degree in accounting, or save $10,000 within three years for a down payment on a house." This procedure removes us from vague generalities and establishes specific targets toward which we can direct our energies.

It is imperative that you write your goals down. This helps crystallize your thinking and aids in making them concrete and specific. Otherwise, the goals remain vague and abstract.

In the space below take approximately fifteen

minutes and write your lifetime goals. You'll want to interpret these goals from your present perspective. As you write these lifetime goals, consider at least these important areas: personal, physical, financial, social, intellectual, spiritual, family, career, and community.

LIFETIME GOALS

1.

2.

3.

4.

5.

6.

7.

8.

Because most people have not been involved in any type of goal-setting workshop, they write most of their goals in very general terms. For example, they include such things as wanting to make more money, enjoying more happiness, becoming a better salesman, or achieving more success.

Next, I'd like for you to take fifteen minutes and write in the space below the specific goals you plan to achieve in the next three years.

THREE-YEAR GOALS

1.

2.

3.

4.

5.

6.

7.

8.

It's time now to write the specific goals you are going to achieve during the next six months. As you write your goals, avoid using the words "more" or "better." When either of these terms is used, the goal is probably not nearly as specific as it should be. In the space provided below, write your goals for the next six months.

SIX-MONTH GOALS

1.

2.

3.

4.

5.

6.

7.

8.

Each of your goals carries a different value. Some are more important than others. Because this is true, you'll want to go back over your Lifetime, Three-Year, and Six-Month goals and rank them by priority. From each list place the number "1" beside the most important goal on that list, the number "2" beside the next most important goal, and continue until you have placed a number beside each goal on your different lists. This procedure is very necessary because it helps you identify those goals which are the most important and on which you should spend more time. It also breaks each goal down into achievable activities.

But how are goals achieved? Goals are achieved through activities. These activities are simply steps you'll be taking along the way toward achieving your goals. For example, one of your goals may have been to insure financial security. Your activities to achieve that goal might be to purchase one hundred dollars worth of stock each month, place one hundred dollars in the bank each month, or invest a certain amount in real estate.

In the space below, write your top three Lifetime Goals. Under each goal write as many activities as you can that will help you achieve each goal.

LIFETIME GOALS and ACTIVITIES

Lifetime Goal #1

Activities:

A.

B.

C.

D.

E.

Lifetime Goal #2

Activities

A.

B.

C.

D.

E.

Lifetime Goal #3

Activities
A.

B.

C.

D.

E.

THREE-YEAR GOALS and ACTIVITIES

Goal #1

Activities:
A.

B.

C.

D.

E.

Goal #2

Activities

A.

B.

C.

D.

E.

Goal #3

Activities

A.

B.

C.

D.

E.

F.

G.

H.

You can always go back and revise your goals or activities according to your needs and desires. You have written these on paper, not in concrete. Our goals change as our values change. You'll also find it necessary sometimes to modify your activities to achieve your goals. Such modification usually indicates growth on your part.

Periodically I find it helpful to ask during the day, "What am I doing with my time right now?" You will find it beneficial to write this question on a three-by-five index card and leave it on your desk, put it in your pocket, tape it to the refrigerator door, or place it in some prominent location where you can see it as a reminder. It can help you reflect on the activities on which you need to spend your time to accomplish your goals.

All your waking minutes should not be spent in activities to achieve your top few priority goals. You need time to do things which relax, inform, or entertain you. You need time to be you. The amount of "free" time varies with each of us. If your schedule seems to stay full most of the time, you will probably need to schedule some time for recreational activities. Your feelings of accomplishment will be greater as you develop a well-rounded schedule which meets your personal needs.

Perhaps there are some additional strengths which you need to develop that will help you achieve your goals. Do you need to become more enthusiastic, develop a more positive attitude, organize your time better, reduce your food consumption, quit smoking, or become more flexible? Please continue your efforts toward a more rewarding and productive life by completing the following exercise.

STRENGTHS I NEED TO DEVELOP

1. Attitudes I Need to Develop:

   A.

   B.

   C.

   D.

   E.

2. Skills I Need to Develop:

   A.

B.

C.

D.

E.

3. Habits I Need to Develop:

A.

B.

C.

D.

E.

It's a fair question for you to ask: "Does this goal-setting process work?" Thousands of people who have used it say that it does! It has worked effectively in my life. This process has helped me achieve more things in my life than I ever dreamed of achieving. For more than twenty years I have researched the lives of successful people. They were goal-oriented individuals. They knew where they wanted to go, what they wanted to achieve, and when they wanted to arrive. They were achievement-oriented people. They could visualize exactly what they wanted. And they asked this important question: "What am I willing to give up in order to achieve my goals?" They also asked, "Is the gain worth the pain?" As a graduate student in one of my classes, Debbie Gallimore, used to say, "Dr. Garner, those questions are *heavy!*"

Let me share with you a few examples which, I believe, validate this goal-setting process. One fellow in my class named Bob Carter set a goal to earn $25,000 a year within a three-year period. He wrote down the activities he was going to use to make his goals a reality. One of his activities, incidentally, was to get another job. Within three years he was earning over $50,000 a year, and this year he will probably earn over $100,000. As they say in Texas, "That ain't all bad!" Bob decided that the "gain was worth the pain." His goals were very clear, and the daily visualization of these goals motivated him to achieve them. Bob made a move to improve, and it paid off. America is a country in which this can be done. God bless America!

A lady in another goal-setting workshop set a goal to earn a college degree in early childhood education within a five-year period. This middle-aged lady had never entered college, and she planned to go part time so that she could meet the needs of her family. This lady, Joe McKenzie, will receive her degree this year from a major university.

Another lady, Joan Lee, used goal-setting to achieve an important objective in her life. She specified the goal to become a director within a certain time in Transart Industries. She listed the activities she needed to engage in, ranked them by priority, and took action. Today she is a director in this fine business.

It's extremely important to keep our eyes on our goals. Let it be our magnificent obsession. We think about it constantly. We have to achieve it. We really want it. It hits our hot button! In the goal-setting workshops I conduct, participants have found it very helpful to get a piece of poster board and glue on it some pictures or symbols which remind them of their goals. You, too, should get a detailed picture of the kind of house you plan to own, or of the clothes you plan to purchase, or of the car you are going to buy, or the college from which you plan to graduate, or the kind of career you plan to pursue. You'll want to divide this poster into three sections, which include Lifetime Goals, Three-Year Goals, and Six-Month Goals.

Several times each day you will be motivated toward achieving your goals as you look at pictures of things you plan to achieve. My mother used to say, "Out of sight, out of mind."

Have you ever heard the name "Gerry Dorsey"? Probably not very many people have. He was a singer who wanted to have a successful career entertaining audiences. He spent several years singing in small night clubs, then decided to make some changes. He found a new manager. The manager was unable to book him anywhere because his name was associated with failure. The manager decided to change Gerry's name. Within four years he became a superstar—and a millionaire. He had changed his name to "Engelbert Humperdinck."

Sometimes we have to try another way to reach our goals. Although one road may have an insurmountable obstacle, there are other roads which can lead us to our goals. God never closes one door without opening two more. Faith can move mountains. Winning requires persistent faith.

It is important to picture your goals as though they had already been achieved. Picture yourself *being, doing, or having something*—a *fait accompli*. Avoid picturing the individual steps you think should be taken to achieve what you desire. Because your conscious mind is limited by your five physical senses, it cannot know the best direction to take. Your subconscious mind operates twenty-four hours every day on all levels and in all directions. It does not have the limitations that are characteristic of the conscious mind.

In his book, *One More Step*, James Dillet Freeman has included a challenge to all of us:

> A hill is not too hard to climb
> Taken one step at a time.
> One step is not too much to take;
> One try is not too much to make.
> One step, one try, one song, one smile
> Will shortly stretch into a mile.
> And everything worthwhile was done
> By small steps taken one by one.
> To reach the goal you started for,
> Take one step more . . . take one step more.

WISDOM FROM WINNERS

WINNERS can take a negative environment and make it a training camp for personal growth.

WINNERS see something positive in everything that happens.

WINNERS develop the ability to see difference where others see only likeness, and likeness where others see only difference.

WINNERS believe the best angle from which to approach any problem is the try-angle.

WINNERS hold a picture of what they want to happen, while losers hold a picture of what they don't want to happen.

WINNERS believe that a specific goal is a dream being acted upon.

WINNERS ask, "What am I willing to give, or give up, to achieve my goals?"

WINNERS believe that obstacles are the things you see when you take your eyes off your goals.

CHAPTER 6

Releasing Your Untapped Potential

You don't have to be sick to get better.

Walt Disney conceptualized an amusement park that families could enjoy on special vacations together. He dreamed of a park filled with Tomorrowland adventures, Adventureland jungles, Frontierland memories, and Fantasyland dreams. The kids could journey into the world of the future, take jungle cruises on boats, ride Western mine trains, and also enjoy cotton candy, ice-cream bars, and popcorn as they saw storybook tales "come to life."

Guess what? Disney's close associates advised him to forget his dream. They told him it would never go over. They said it would cost too much, there wasn't a good location available on which to build it, and the time was not right. I'm glad Walt Disney did not listen to his associates. They were unable to see the mental picture Disney had. Perhaps they had tunnel vision, or maybe they weren't willing to take a risk.

Victor Hugo said, "Nothing is so powerful as an idea whose time has come." This was true in the life of Walt Disney. You see, he never gave up on his dream—and I hope you won't either.

If all possible objections must first be overcome, nothing will be attempted. Andre Gide said, "We cannot discover new oceans unless we are courageous to lose sight of the shore." Too many people are "waiting for their ships to come in, when they haven't sent any ships out." Some are waiting for their college degrees, when they haven't enrolled in any courses.

The "Magic Kingdom" was opened in 1955. Disney said, "Disneyland will never be completed. It will continue to grow as long as there is imagination left in the world."

Frequently, the most difficult part of climbing the ladder of success is getting through the crowd at the bottom. Most of the people in these crowds are living lives of mediocrity and they get up each morning hoping something good is going to happen to them that day. The winners are out there taking risks and making things happen. They realize that opportunity's knock may come only once or twice. And they're willing to act on their dreams. As former president Ronald Reagan said, "Every new day begins with possibilities."

Psychologist Dr. Dudley Calvert tells the story of a railway employee who accidentally locked himself in a refrigerator car. He was unable to escape and couldn't attract the attention of those outside, so he resigned himself to his fate. As he felt his body becoming numb, he recorded the story of his approaching death in sentences scribbled on the wall of the car. "I'm becoming colder," he wrote, "still colder, now. Nothing to do but wait . . . I am slowly freezing to death . . . half asleep now, I can hardly write." And finally, "These may be my last words."

And they were, for when the car was opened they found him dead. Yet the temperature of the car was fifty-six degrees! The freezing apparatus had been out of order. There was no physical reason for his death. There was plenty of air . . . he hadn't suffocated. He was the victim of his own illusion. His conclusions were all wrong! He was so sure he knew!

Too many people live a life of mediocrity. Think how many people get to the end of their lives and say, "I got a lot out of life." But think how precious few people get to the end of life and are able to say, "I put a lot into life!"

You see, the real tragedy of life is not in being limited to a few talents, but in the failure to use those talents. It's not who we are that holds us back—it's who we think we're not. We need to realize that our pasts do not limit our possibilities. Psychologists indicate that most of us only develop and utilize about 10 to 15 percent of our potential.

President Woodrow Wilson did not learn the alphabet until he was nine years old. He didn't read until he was eleven, and he was considered dull by members of his family. Gen. George Patton was twelve years old before he could read. Vice-President Nelson Rockefeller was plagued throughout his school years by his inability to spell and read. And yet he graduated cum laude from Dartmouth College and earned a Phi Beta Kappa key.

Don't beat up on yourself. Some of the worst demotivators in the English language are the words, "I should have . . . I could have . . . I would have." Why not make a concerted effort to eliminate these from our vocabulary? Instead, let's say, "Next time, I'll . . ."

Situations in life make some people better and others bitter—depending on their attitude. I am convinced that life is 10 percent what actually happens to me and 90 percent how I react to it. A friend of mine said, "Art, I don't have good days. I create good days."

Josh Billings once said, "Human beings have always employed an enormous variety of clever devices for running away from themselves." We manage to imprison ourselves in a comfortable web we weave around ourselves. Sometimes it takes a major change such as death, marriage, divorce, a move to another city, or a job change to break the pattern of our lives. Today we fill our lives with diversions, become involved with so many people, and pack our minds with so much knowledge that we rarely take the time to probe the world within.

Self-renewal means keeping the horizons wide by becoming versatile and adaptive. Self-renewing individuals are not trapped by routine, fixed habits, and attitudes. As years go by we narrow the scope and variety of life. We select a few friends. Our minds become made up. Our opinions harden. Soon this becomes our world of imprisonment. We become apathetic to our surroundings. Travel and education are effective means of teaching self-renewal.

Individuals who are self-renewing are capable of accepting and giving love. The joys and sufferings of those individuals we love help enrich our lives. Love and friendship force us to have a new perspective and help dissolve the rigidities of the isolated self.

I'd like to give you some questions that will help you identify and analyze what you consider important in life and help you reflect on what you may wish to change.

1. Do you spend an adequate amount of time feeding your mind positive thoughts, ideas, and knowledge?
2. Do you believe and understand that success is personal and that you must look at the end of your own arm for a helping hand?
3. What are your three strongest personal assets or abilities?
4. Have you been fully utilizing these personal assets or abilities?
5. Do you allow fear to discourage you from trying new experiences to learn, grow, or improve your skills?
6. Do you spend an inordinate amount of time procrastinating?

7. Do you take special training courses or programs to improve yourself professionally?
8. What things give you the greatest satisfaction where you work?
9. What would success really mean to you, personally?
10. Do you associate with successful people in your professional field?
11. Are your decisions and opinions based on intuition, or upon research, analysis, and thought?
12. What new activities and interests would you like to explore in the next year?
13. Do most of the television programs you watch either entertain or enlighten you?
14. Do you need to rebudget your time and change some habits to make better use of your time?

Your sincerity in answering these fourteen questions will help you assess where you are now and where you'd like to go in your personal and professional life.

When life kicks you, let it kick you forward. Anyone can start but only a Thoroughbred will finish. Growth always brings change. Although we often feel uncomfortable with change, we must remember that it is the only thing that has brought progress.

The mother eagle has to force her young to leave the nest and fly. The eaglet would rather stay in the nest and be fed and cared for. But if it remains in the nest, it will never use its great wings or enjoy the great heights for which it was created. The mother eagle, therefore, has to knock it out of the nest, catch it on her great wings if it falls too far, and do this until it learns to fly on its own.

It's easy for us to become very comfortable in our nests. It takes guts to leave the ruts. Significant progress has been made for humanity because of the people who have been willing to leave the ruts and chart new paths, make great inventions, or solve some scientific or medical mystery. Someone has said that the major difference between a rut and a grave is that the grave has two ends to it and the rut just goes on and on.

Even if you don't feel good, act as though you do, and you will probably soon begin to feel better. That's the way it works for most of us. Researchers have now ascertained that a smile— even if it is forced—triggers an intricate series of responses throughout the body, all of which conspire to make us feel better. I like what Mary Kay Ash, the founder of Mary Kay Cosmetics, says in her new book, *Mary Kay on People Management:* "Fake it 'til you make it."

Mark Twain once said, "If a cat sits on a hot stove, that cat will never sit on a 'hot' stove again." He continued, "In fact, that cat will never sit on a 'cold' stove, either." That cat will associate stoves with a bad, hot experience and say, "Never again." This is another example of how we, like the cat, encounter a "bad experience" and then penalize ourselves by putting "lids" on our untapped potential.

Two men were sitting on a park bench watching a squirrel jump from one high tree to another. The squirrel appeared to be aiming for a limb so far out of reach that the leap looked like suicide. It would miss, but it always had a safe landing on another branch below. It would then climb to its goal and appear satisfied.

The old man remarked to the young one, "I have seen lots of squirrels jump like that, especially if predators are around, and they don't ever hit the ground. A lot of them miss the limb they are aiming for, but I've never seen any get hurt in trying." Then he laughed and observed, "I guess they have got to at least take a risk or they would remain in one tree all their lives."

After that experience, whenever the young man had to choose between risking a new situation or hanging back, he visualized the old man on the park bench saying, "They've got to risk it if they don't want to spend their lives in one tree." The younger man thought to himself . . . if a squirrel takes chances . . . have I less nerve than a squirrel?

An interesting and historic city to visit is New Orleans. My wife and I enjoy eating those famous beignets at Cafe Du Monde. We then walk past the oldest standing cathedral in the United States, the St. Louis Cathedral. It is located on Jackson Square. The citizens so named this beautiful spot because of Andrew Jackson's assistance in winning the Battle of New Orleans during the War of 1812. If you've visited there, you've probably seen the statue of President Jackson that stands in the middle of the park surrounded by beautiful flowers.

Because of the large number of tourists who visit Jackson Square, many vendors, artists, and musicians set up their little shops on the sidewalks. Many people like to sit on the park benches, enjoy the Southern sun, and watch people walk by.

The story is told that large crowds were gathering to observe the skill with which a talented artist painted tourist portraits. A beggar saw this as an opportunity to rattle his cup and attract the attention of a few sympathetic visitors. The beggar spent the day shaking the coins in his tin cup.

As the sun was going down behind the silhouettes of the large buildings, the artist started cleaning his brushes and storing his supplies for the night. The beggar saw the tourist crowds dwindling and decided it was time for him to leave also. The beggar walked toward the artist's little stand. As he passed by, he stopped to glance at some of the portraits the artist had painted that day.

The beggar saw a portrait of a healthy, successful-looking man. He looked at the artist and asked, "Who is that fellow?" The artist replied with an amused smile, "That's the you I see."

The beggar was shocked. He stood there for a few minutes staring at the portrait. Then he said to the artist, "If you can see me that way, then that's the me I can become." The beggar raised his head high, threw his shoulders back, smiled, and walked away—never to return as a beggar at Jackson Square.

Developing a positive view of the self is not an easy task. It requires a great deal of personal effort and concentrated work. It is a task that is never complete. It is, as psychologist Abraham Maslow said, "a constant struggle to climb to the mountain top and touch fingers with God."

Optimistic people seem to view change and adjustment as opportunities for renewal and for revitalizing their sense of well-being. These positive people can assess their strengths and weaknesses realistically. They enhance their strengths and take actions to improve their weaknesses.

WINNERS understand their feelings. They accept stress and uncertainty as part of the price they pay for living on this earth as they develop their potential. They control their feelings instead of having their feelings control them. And they keep growing and reaching out for new and satisfying experiences. Such people are open, strong, optimistic, and happy.

Psychologists tell us that the most dangerous emotion is self-pity. The most helpful and powerful emotion is self-value. Self-pity inhibits creativity and productivity. It reminds me of someone applying the brake in the car with one foot while pushing the accelerator down with the other foot. It's difficult, if not impossible, to move forward. A tremendous amount of energy and potential is lost.

Here are some strategies that will help us develop our potential and accept change as a satisfying challenge.

1. **Learn to see the big picture.**
2. **Internalize the belief that we have more capabilities, power, and potential than we ever use.**

3. **Learn to accept stress and temporary set-backs.**
4. **Learn to use time constructively.**
5. **Develop the ability to motivate ourselves into positive action.**
6. **Learn to set and achieve goals.**
7. **Learn to communicate effectively with ourselves and others.**
8. **Learn to negotiate with the circumstances of living and working.**

Now let's use this chapter to discuss each of these strategies in detail.

We must learn to see the big picture. We can choose to live in a cave or build a house with a view. It is important to develop a sense of wholeness with our lives. This means that we will look at the sum total of our successes and failures—not just where we are today. We must have a perspective of all that we have done, not just what happened at two o'clock on Wednesday afternoon. Each of us has accomplished many things, worked hard, made contributions, enjoyed the sweet taste of success—even when today may not seem like a successful one.

It is important that we judge ourselves with a sense of history and not by the present moment alone. Although it may seem that we're in a cave one day, it does not mean that we are denied the sunshine, the stars, and the achievements of previous days. It helps to have a gestalt view—a view of a whole existence—and not a fragmented view of daily events. The big picture tells us that we are worthy, that we are capable, and that life is meaningful.

There is a story of a Wisconsin pumpkin farmer who was walking through his field one day when he came across a small glass jug. Out of curiosity he poked a young pumpkin vine through the neck of the glass jug. The vine began to grow inside the glass jug until one day a small pumpkin appeared. The pumpkin grew until it became only as large as the jug itself.

Let's compare ourselves and our self-image to the pumpkin in the glass jar. We place limits on ourselves in that we each have painted a mental picture of "self." Our actions and emotions are usually consistent with our self-image. We believe in this picture we paint of self and we don't question its validity.

People who see themselves as failures will usually behave in ways to fail—no matter how hard they try to succeed. Those who see themselves as unlucky seem to find ways to prove their "bad luck."

The mental picture we paint can be a barrier standing between what we can accomplish and what we don't accomplish. Most of the time we underestimate our potential. We each need to paint a bigger picture of "self." Until we paint a bigger pictrre we will only grow as big as our limits (or our jug) will allow.

The famous plastic surgeon and author Dr. Maxwell Maltz said, "One is never too young or too old to change the self-image. It is never too late to start a more productive and creative life."

Recently, I went to the Silverton Resort, which is north of Seattle, to give a speech to the Washington Society of Radiologic Technologists. The second day I was there, I was standing on the fourth floor waiting for an elevator so I could go down to the restaurant on the first floor. An elderly gentleman walked up and was waiting with me for the elevator. I said, "Good morning, sir. How are you doing?" He looked at me, smiled, and said, "Young man, every day above ground is a good day." What a beautiful philosophy with which to face the world each day.

The late Sen. Hubert Humphrey from Minnesota said that the worst moment in his life was the day he discovered he had cancer. He refused to think of himself as a statistic. He knew there would be days of pain and struggle, but he geared himself to fight and win. His faith and hope carried him from day to day.

Senator Humphrey said that the game is over if you don't overcome self-pity. His father impressed on him that there was no time for self-pity in life. He remembered the challenges and adversities his family experienced on the plains of South Dakota. Those memories included the blizzards, dust storms, summer heat, and droughts. When the crops failed they were future-oriented enough to believe that another year was coming. And he remembered when they had to sell the family farm in order to pay the bills.

He believed the biggest mistake people made was giving up. He said that adversity is an experience, not a final act. Life has always been a struggle. If anything is easy, it probably isn't worthwhile. When the senator was feeling low, he would draw strength from the prayer of St. Francis of Assisi. Part of it reads, "Where there is doubt, let me sow faith; where there is despair, hope; where there is darkness, light; and where there is sadness, joy."

Stop looking back. Life for many people is made miserable because their time is spent in self-pity over unfulfilled desires or unrealized ambition. "Oh, if I could only live my life over again, I wouldn't make the same mistakes twice." Of course not; you would make a whole set of new ones! In living, it's important to remember that the longer the time you stay young, the shorter the time you will be old.

The following poem can inspire us to "hang in there" in the pursuit of our dreams and goals.

FRIENDLY OBSTACLES

For every hill I've had to climb,
For every stone that bruised my feet,
For all the blood and sweat and grime,
For blinding storms and burning heat,
My heart sings but a grateful song—
These are the things that made me strong.
For all the heartaches and the tears,
For all the anguish and the pain,
For gloomy days and fruitless years,
And for the hopes that lived in vain,
I do give thanks, for now I know
These were the things that helped me grow!
'Tis not the softer things of life,
Which stimulate our will to strive.

But bleak adversity and strife
Do most to keep our will alive.
O'er rose-strewn paths the weaklings creep,
But brave hearts dare to climb the steep.

—Author Unknown

If we learn to see the big picture, we can withstand any setbacks.

Now let's consider the second strategy: internalizing the belief that we have more power than we ever use. Each of us has vast untapped resources. Call it the power of positive thinking. Call it yoga. Call it meditation. Call it spiritual growth. Call it whatever you wish. Each of us has more to give than we have ever given. Each of us has more skill, strength, power, ideas, or wisdom than anyone has ever asked of us. The important thing in life is not what we have—it's what we do with what we have.

Herbert Otto says, "We are all functioning at a small fraction of our capacity to live fully in its total meaning of loving, caring, creating and adventuring. Consequently, the actualizing of our potential can become the most exciting adventure in our lifetime."

For some people, getting out of a rut is the highest mountain they will ever have to climb. I remember the cartoon that pictured two people walking in a ditch that came up to their shoulders. The person in front turned to the person following close behind and said, "Yes, I know we're in a rut, but on the other hand, it is very comfortable." The rut is comfortable because it is predictable. It gives us stability and security. If we do the same things today that we have done for the past five years, we can predict the results . . . and that gives us stability.

The tragedy of life is not death, but what dies inside us while we live. You have probably known people who "retired long before they retired at work." Tell yourself over and over again that you're not going to sit by and be bored with life. WINNERS approach life with the attitude that they would rather "wear out through using their talents and abilities than rust out from sitting on the sidelines and watching life go by."

> Yesterday is a canceled check.
> Tomorrow is a promissory note.
> Today is ready cash. Use it!

My good friend Betty Goff Cartwright has traveled to more than 250 countries around the world. She shared with me how the glorious statue of David, sculpted by the master sculptor Michelangelo, was carved from one huge block of granite weighing over ten tons. This same piece of granite was considered a reject a century before. It was labeled as unfit for a work of sculpture. Yet out of this rejected piece of granite was fashioned a masterpiece in the hands of a world-renowned sculptor.

Learning is an absolute survival skill in today's highly competitive and changing world. Oliver W. Holmes said, "Even if you are on the right track, you'll get run over if you just sit there." Willingness to learn provides "employment security," not "job security." Job security is probably a thing of the past in most businesses and industries today. The more you know, the greater your market value will be to more people. Knowledge is a combination of education and experience. It is important to know how to apply and utilize the knowledge we possess.

Learning is a springboard to success. If you don't like the person you are, you can change through learning. Be excited about learning. The only ones afraid to learn are those who are afraid they won't improve. As Ronald E. Osborn said, "Unless you try to do something beyond what you have already mastered, you will never grow."

Harry and Ada Mae Day lived in a four-room adobe house that had no running water, no electricity, and no school within driving distance. When his father died, Harry had to take over the operation of the ranch. Although he could not attend Stanford University as he had wanted to, he dreamed that one day his daughter would go there. Ada Mae taught the children at home using newspapers, magazines, and books. One summer they took their children to all the state capitols west of the Mississippi River.

Years later their daughter did attend Stanford, graduated from law school, and went on to become the first woman justice on the U.S. Supreme Court. Much of the credit for Sandra Day O'Connor's success goes to a determined ranch mother sitting in her adobe house, reading to her children by the hour and who, with her husband, scampered up the stairways of capitol domes, their children in tow.

Heather Whitestone, a twenty-one-year-old student from Birmingham, Alabama, is the first Miss

America with a disability. After receiving a diph-theria-pertussis-tetanus shot when she was one and one-half years old, she became deaf. She lost 95 percent of her hearing and relies on lip reading, sign language, and a hearing aid to help her communicate effectively in a hearing world.

Shortly after her reign began as the 1995 Miss America, Heather had to face reporters at a press conference. She asked reporters to stop flashing their cameras so fast so she could have time to process reading the lips of her questioners. She said, "Exclusive use of sign language limits what the hearing impaired can achieve."

Heather says, "The most handicapped person in the world is a negative thinker." Her mother has been credited for encouraging her daughter from early childhood not to give up because she has a hearing loss. She used encouraging statements such as: "The last four letters of 'American' spells 'I can.'"

Heather won the preliminary talent contest by performing a two-and-one-half-minute ballet routine to "Via Dolorosa" by feeling the vibrations from the music. Her inspiring life is a beautiful example of what can be done to develop and utilize one's potential.

Do you know how to train fleas? It's an easy skill to learn. Eileen Pritchard told me how to do it. You go to a friend's house and pick some fleas off the dog. Put these fleas into a gallon jar. Then screw the lid on it. You can then observe the fleas jumping and hitting the jar lid. They do this over and

over. And then they give up. They won't try any-
more—because they are not convinced that they
will ever be able to get out of that jar. You can then
remove the jar lid and never have to wonder about
the fleas escaping. You see—the fleas have imposed
upon themselves limitations that they will never
overcome. The fleas are fully convinced that they
have reached the height of their jumping potential. And besides, they don't want any more
"headaches" from hitting the jar lid.

Margaret Rhea Seddon is a pioneer who has pursued a goal since she was twelve years old. That is
when she decided she wanted to become an astro-
naut. She is one of NASA's new breed for a new
adventure in space—a breed that includes women
in a challenging and rewarding career.

She was born and raised in Murfreesboro, Tennessee. Her family has been there for five generations. Her mother and father encouraged her to
do things well and to believe that there wasn't anything she couldn't do if she set her mind to it.
After high school graduation she enrolled at the
University of California at Berkeley because of the
excellent undergraduate program they had in sci-
ence.

Margaret's strong determination and optimistic
spirit helped her accumulate a steady stream of
achievements. After completing an undergraduate
degree at Berkeley, she completed her medical program at the University of Tennessee College of
Health Sciences. She also pursued her hobby of flying airplanes. Dr. Seddon was selected as one of

the thirty-five new astronauts to begin training for the shuttle program. She probably smiled several times from the spacecraft as she looked down on Murfreesboro and remembered her parents and friends living there. She had used her talents to the best of her ability to get where she was.

Joe Girard was named the world's number-one salesman for twelve consecutive years and also named in *The Guinness Book of World Records* as the world's greatest salesman. His career was not without many obstacles. Early in his career he invested everything he owned in a construction business, and someone swindled him. At the age of thirty-five he hit rock bottom, and considered himself a failure. He was bankrupt. The bank was threatening to repossess his house and car. The bill collectors were knocking at his door trying to get their money. His children were hungry and his wife was disappointed and angry because of his inability to get a job and provide for their family.

One day as Joe was inside his home pretending not to be there, a bill collector stood outside his front door to collect money that Joe owed his company. This event and the events that followed would change the course of Joe Girard's life. On his knees as he prayed that day, he vowed if God would help him, he would help other people. He had not been very honest in his dealings with people up to this time. He felt that God had all he could handle of Joe Girard. He was willing to change his life for the better.

The next day Joe talked the manager of a local

Chevrolet agency into giving him a chance as a salesman. This was the first week in January, not the best month for car sales. He called every person he knew and asked each one to buy a car from him. Fifteen minutes before closing, a man came into the showroom. Joe practically begged him to buy a car from him. The man was impressed with his sincerity and did so.

Joe became confident in his sales ability in the months that followed. He began to believe in himself. He started selling more cars than anyone in the entire showroom. His only real plan for selling was to work longer and harder than any other salesperson in the agency. He was inspired by his need to provide for his family, his need to get out of debt, and his need to prove to his father that he could be somebody.

One of the grand things about life is one's ability to succeed in spite of difficulties or handicaps. If you have confidence in yourself and your potential abilities, don't let anybody talk you out of them. Make sure you are right, then go ahead.

F. W. Woolworth was once hired as a janitor for fifty cents a day by a retail-store owner who didn't think Woolworth had enough business sense to wait on customers.

Marconi, the inventor of the radio, was reprimanded by his father for wasting time when he first began to experiment with the radio.

When Thomas Edison was in school, he was always at the bottom of his class because he couldn't remember his three R's. His teachers called him stupid and doctors predicted he would have brain trouble.

The first time George Gershwin ever played piano onstage, he was laughed out of the theater by both the audience and his fellow actors.

When Zane Grey was still an unknown, trying to sell his book manuscripts, a publisher told him he had no ability for writing fiction.

Louisa May Alcott *(Little Women)* was a tomboy marked by the people in her town as a girl who would never amount to very much. A publisher once told her to give up the idea of writing.

First impressions of talents, abilities, and aptitudes are sometimes grossly inaccurate. Just because something appears to be deficient doesn't make it so. You may have talents buried under feelings of inadequacy and unpreparedness that could be working right now in both your personal and professional lives. Abilities are developed by exercise and use.

Harry Truman once said, "A winner never quits." And that is true. Real WINNERS never perch on a plateau—they are always climbing higher.

Imagine four chairs in front of us. Let's put a different person in each chair. One cannot talk, one cannot walk, one cannot see, and one cannot hear. In spite of their physical disabilities and other factors, each of these individuals had one thing in common. Each had the "I can" attitude.

1. The first man was born tongue-tied, and could hardly speak. He vowed he would

make his tongue work, for he had something to say. He went out every day into his native forest and practiced to make his tongue work. He went on to become one of the greatest of all Greek orators. Who was this man? Demosthenes.

2. The man in the second chair said, "Even though polio has put me in a wheelchair, I will do something great for this land of mine." Did he? He became governor of New York and was elected president of the United States four times. Who was this man? Franklin D. Roosevelt.

3. The third person felt that, even though he was blind, he could create beautiful pictures in other people's minds. Did he? He wrote such beautiful poems as *Paradise Lost* and *Paradise Regained.* Who was he? John Milton.

4. The fourth person had a fierce belief in himself and said, "Despite the fact that I am deaf, I will put sounds in the ears of others that will last forever." Perhaps within the past few weeks you have been inspired by one of his numerous symphonies. Who was this man? Ludwig van Beethoven.

These examples teach us that individuals with varying levels of challenges, shortcomings, or difficulties can rise above circumstances and make a positive contribution in life. It's not who we are that really counts; it's what we do with who we are. Too many people expend a great deal of energy and time in the "blaming mode." They blame parents, lack of education, social circumstances, and numerous other factors for causing them to be where they are in life. WINNERS take the situations in which they find themselves and look for opportunities to learn and grow. Then they take action to bring about improvement.

You see, the real WINNERS in life are the losers who won't quit trying. I like the attitude of TV talk host Art Linkletter. He said, "Things work out best for the people who make the best out of the way things work out."

Now let's turn to the third strategy: learning to accept stress and temporary setbacks. These things are a natural part of living. The only people who don't experience them are out there in the cemeteries.

Stress is a physical, mental, and emotional response to fear or ambivalence. These responses produce specific bodily reactions. Once they are understood, many of these reactions can be controlled by good physical and mental health.

A regular savings program can help provide for economic security. We can help ensure employment security by reading, studying, and learning new skills. I love the plaque that reads, "You don't have to be sick to get better."

Attitude is an inward feeling that is expressed verbally and nonverbally. Our attitudes are often contagious. Have you ever noticed what happens to a group of people when one person expresses a negative attitude? We've also noticed the lift received when someone expresses a positive attitude of acceptance and understanding.

The future looks bright when the attitude is right, and whether we are twelve, twenty-five, or sixty-five years old, our attitudes toward life are still under construction. When the going gets tough, it's important to remember that what really matters is what happens in us, not to us! We become what we think about. What we think about, we bring about.

Dr. G. Campbell Morgan used to tell about a businessman in Chicago whose building burned completely to the ground. The next morning this courageous businessman arrived at the ruins carrying a table. He set the table up in the middle of the debris. Above the table he had scribbled an optimistic sign that read, "Everything lost except wife, children, and hope. Business will resume as usual tomorrow morning."

The story of Wilma Rudolph is an inspiration to anyone. She was one of the greatest runners in American track history. She achieved success over a staggering disability. For one-third of her life she was unable to walk. Wilma was the seventeenth child in her family. Although her parents didn't have a lot of money, they had a lot of faith and love. In fact, Wilma said that her mother made her believe in herself.

While living with her family in Clarksville, Tennessee, Wilma was stricken with scarlet fever and double pneumonia. For weeks this small girl lay near death. Finally, she pulled through, but her left leg had suffered a form of paralysis. Her mother wrapped her in a blanket and took her by bus to a medical school in Nashville. After conducting numerous tests on her legs, the specialists concluded that it would take years of daily massaging the leg to restore it to some use. The doctors taught her mother how to massage her leg.

On her day off each week, Wilma's mother took her to Nashville for special treatment. She did this for the next two years. This special treatment included heat and water therapy. Each day after work and after preparing the family dinner, her mother massaged the wasted little leg until long after Wilma had fallen asleep. Before long Mrs. Rudolph taught three older children to massage, and they began four daily shifts of "rubbing Wilma."

By the time she was eight, Wilma was able to walk with a leg brace. Then she progressed to an orthopedic shoe. She began playing a little basketball with her brothers. In high school, she went out for girls' basketball and track. The girls' track coach from Tennessee State University saw her run in a track meet and invited her to try out for a track scholarship.

When Wilma went home and told her family, her mother said, "You're the first one in this house to ever have the chance to go to college. If running is going to do that, I want you to set your mind to be the best. Never give up!" In the coming years, Wilma remembered those words, "Never give up!" many times. While she was in college she became ill and had to have her tonsils removed. These infected tonsils had been sapping her strength for a long time. Three weeks later she set a record in the 200-meter race.

In Rome, Italy she set a new Olympic record of eleven seconds in the 100-meter women's sprint. The next day she won the 200-meter trials. Then, in the finals, she blazed to a breath-stopping victory in the 200-meter race. She became a triple gold medalist for the United States.

Later, when she returned home to a heroine's welcome, schools and businesses were closed as people lined the streets to cheer their champion. Wilma had a burning desire to win and she was willing to pay the price of preparing to win. Five-time Olympian Willye White, Rudolph's friend for almost forty years, said, "She had a winning spirit. She was always coming back from impossible odds."

Wilma Rudolph died at age fifty-four in the fall of 1994. Cancer proved to be the one obstacle she could not overcome.

Name ten successful people you know about. Probably each one of these ten failed many times in striving to achieve their dreams. But they didn't give up. Most of us fell 240 times when we first were taught to walk. I'm glad we kept on trying. A friend of mine is always saying, "Don't give in, don't give out, don't give over, and don't give up. Just keep giving the best that you can."

Recently, someone shared with me the beautiful parable of Sadhu Sundar Singh. He was a Hindu who was converted to Christianity and later became a missionary in India. Late one afternoon he was walking with a Buddhist monk through the Himalayas. Darkness was approaching and the air was turning very cold. The monk told Sadhu that they could easily freeze to death if they didn't reach the monastery before nightfall.

As they were walking near a ravine, they heard someone down in the ravine crying for help. Someone had apparently fallen down the cliff and could not climb back up. The monk said, "Let's not stop. God has brought this man to his fate. He must work it out for himself. If we don't hurry, we'll freeze to death."

Sadhu replied, "God has sent me here to help this man. I cannot abandon him." The monk went on ahead by himself while Sadhu climbed down the cliff to check on the injured stranger. Because the man's leg was broken, he could not walk. Sadhu took his own blanket, made a sling out of it, and tied the man to his back. Utilizing all the power he had, he barely got the man back up to the narrow path.

He slowly and deliberately walked in the snow with the injured man on his back. Because it was now dark, Sadhu could barely see the path. Several times he was nearly overcome with fatigue. But he kept on pushing himself. As he drew his last reserve of physical energy, he finally saw the dim lights of the monastery.

After taking a few more steps, he stumbled and almost fell to the ground with the stranger still on his back. But it wasn't from exhaustion. He had almost fallen over some object lying on the narrow road. He bent down on one knee and brushed the snow off the object. It was the body of the monk, who had frozen to death. Several years later, someone asked him, "What is the most difficult task in life?" Sadhu quickly replied, "To have no burden to carry."

If you're ever driving through Alabama and you have some spare time, visit the city of Enterprise. It has one of the most unique monuments in the country. The citizens erected a monument to an insect. That's right—an insect! They have a boll weevil carved in stone.

For many years the farmers in that area raised cotton almost exclusively. Then came the boll weevils. In fact, they came by the millions. Those nasty little insects ate the cotton crop before the farmers could pick it. The scientists were unable to solve the dilemma. The farmers had to look for other options. Their search was successful. They would raise peanuts! The area was transformed into the peanut capital of the world. The farmers began to make money again.

The citizens decided to give some unique recognition to that little despised insect that spurred them to build a more prosperous industry. So they erected a statue in honor of that little critter—the boll weevil.

Perhaps it will be helpful, when we are facing a serious problem or challenge, to search for an alternative. Maybe you're trying to grow cotton when you should be a peanut farmer. Maybe it

would be helpful to travel in a different direction—
to plant a different crop. The disappointment
you're experiencing may be your "boll weevil."

Someone has written this inspirational poem
about perseverance.

> I've dreamed many dreams that never came true,
> I've seen them vanish at dawn,
> But I've realized enough of my dreams, thank God,
> To make me want to dream on.
>
> I've prayed many prayers when no answer came,
> Though I waited patient and long,
> But answers have come to enough of my prayers,
> To make me keep praying on.
>
> I've trusted many a friend that failed,
> And left me to weep alone,
> But I've found enough of my friends true blue,
> To make me keep trusting on.
>
> I've sown many seeds that fell by the way,
> For the birds to feed upon,
> But I've held enough golden sheaves in my hand,
> To make me keep sowing on.
>
> I've drained the cup of disappointment and pain,
> And gone many days without song,
> But I've sipped enough nectar from the roses of life,
> To make me want to live on.

Napoleon Hill stated that "every adversity has
within it the seed of an equivalent or greater benefit." If we will view our temporary setbacks as stepping-stones instead of stumbling blocks, we can
build more satisfying and rewarding personal
futures. It's what we bring to life, not what life
brings to us, that really counts. An optimist finds
an opportunity in every difficulty, while a pessimist
finds a difficulty in every opportunity.

Each morning brings us a fresh, new day. We can make of it what we will. Get up each morning on the right side of the mind. The attitude you adopt early each morning determines the kind of day you will have. During each day you will notice that attitude begets atmosphere. Julius Rosenwald, former president of Sears, Roebuck and Company, said, "When life hands you lemons, make lemonade."

The next strategy is to use time constructively. Time is the only thing in the world that is equal for all of us. Each of us has twenty-four hours in a day—no more and no less. We must not allow time to become the scapegoat for not doing what we need or want to do. The simple truth is that too many people spend a great deal of time in useless and unproductive ways. Many people waste time complaining about not having it. Time then controls us instead of being controlled by us.

Time management is a skill that can be learned. This skill is developed and improved just like learning to operate a computer, swim, ride a bicycle, or drive a car.

Our actions determine our feelings just as much as our feelings determine our actions. Procrastination fertilizes fear. It takes action to overcome fear. Theodore Roosevelt wrote, "I have often been afraid, but I wouldn't give in to it. I made myself act as though I was not afraid, and gradually my fear disappeared."

Think for just a moment. Why do we procrastinate? Some people think that procrastination is a built-in genetic deficiency that is incurable like some disease, or that it is a part of their personality.

After years of researching human growth and development and working with hundreds of participants in our time-management seminars, I am totally convinced that it is neither of these.

Procrastination is a habit—and a bad habit at that. It's important to break this habit before it breaks you. And that's why I'm so proud to compliment you for reading this book. You see, really and truly, every person we know procrastinates. Some procrastinate a little, while others procrastinate all the time. You and I want to get a handle on this habit and learn to control it so that we can live and enjoy more productive lives.

I smiled when I read the quotation on the desk of an employee at a local bank. It stated: "I'm going to stop putting things off—starting tomorrow—maybe." And then there was a cartoon in a national newspaper that read, "Never put off 'til tomorrow what you can avoid altogether." Or perhaps you have read the one that says, "If you're going to procrastinate, why not wait until tomorrow to do it?"

Opportunities do not come to those who wait. They are captured by those who dare to attempt. The energy to do something seldom comes until you plunge into the task. This strength comes after you have forced yourself to begin. Hesitancy dissipates your energy.

Now let's consider the fifth strategy: develop the ability to motivate yourself into positive action. This may be the most important of all the strategies that can help us grow and become the people we'd like to be. Without this, the other suggestions will only be weak attempts at positive growth. A daily motto for this could be, "Let's make today the best it can be."

Self-motivation is usually the quality that separates the WINNERS from the losers. Self-motivation is a person's deliberate control over himself or herself. It is self-direction, self-determination, self-control, and self-mastery. It is the powerful springboard from which all other abilities emanate. Thomas H. Huxley wrote, "The most valuable trait that you can acquire is the ability to make yourself do the thing you have to do, when it ought to be done, whether you like it or not."

Airplanes are not designed to taxi down the runway. They are designed to fly high in the sky, above the clouds, above the storms. How many people do you know who spend their lives taxiing down the runway of life, revving their engines, but afraid to take off? We were all designed to fly!

My friend Robert Sneed once told me a story about two frogs that fell into a vat of cream. One of the frogs concluded that it was impossible to get out of that situation. He turned over on his back, folded his legs, and sank to the bottom. The other frog had an optimistic attitude and refused to give up. He continued swimming until the vat of cream turned into butter. The frog then stood on the butter and hopped out. Regardless of the circumstances in which you find yourself, don't give up. When you come to the end of the rope, remember to tie a knot and hang on.

People who have been productive and successful in life are remembered largely for being individuals of action. They had the initiative to get things done. Their native intelligence may have had very little to do with their accomplishments. The extent of their formal education may have only partially contributed to their achievements. Thomas Edison, for example, attended school for only a few months in his life. His 1,094 inventions suggest that he was a man of action. He had some ideas and did something with them. Sam Rayburn has well said, "Readiness for opportunity makes for success. Opportunity often comes by accident; readiness never does."

Dr. Harry E. Fosdick once shared a valuable lesson in living successfully. While a young boy he was sent by his mother to pick a quart of raspberries. At first he rebelled against going. Then a new idea came. It would be fun to pick two quarts of raspberries and surprise her. The family was amazed when he returned with two quarts. He learned that we can change any situation by changing our attitude toward it. Nobody ever finds life worth living. One must make it worth living. Life has always been a struggle, but the secret of living is the same today as it has always been. Find a high purpose and build your life around it. Give yourself to it with all your heart.

Young physicians came from across the country to observe the skills of a famous New York surgeon. One young doctor asked to talk to him. The surgeon invited him back to the scrub room. The young doctor told him that they were taught in certain surgical procedures to tie one knot securely. The wise surgeon told him that he had practiced tying three knots for many years. He continued, "I'll let you in on a little secret. Those are my sleeping knots . . . those other two. Tonight I will awake in the middle of the night and wonder if my patients are okay. Remembering that I tied not one or two but three knots, I will lie back and go to sleep. And I will let you in on another secret. In all your life, when you are required to tie one knot, tie two or three and you will come to know more happiness than under any other circumstances."

A prominent salesman summed up his success in three simple words: "And then some." "I discovered at an early age," he said, "that most of the differences between average and top people can be explained in three words. The top people did what was expected of them . . . and then some. They were considerate of others; they were thoughtful and kind . . . and then some. They met their obligations and responsibilities fairly and squarely . . . and then some. They could be counted on in an emergency . . . and then some."

Albert Rogers, who shines shoes in a large New York hotel, polishes and shines with such a sparkle that it almost hurts your eyes. Someone asked him, "Don't you ever get tired?" "No," he replied, "but I would if I just shined shoes." Albert had discovered the secret that makes anything he does pay off in terms of greater satisfaction and a deeper self-realization.

Sometimes we are hesitant to take action because of the fear of criticism. The galleries are full of critics. They play no ball. They make no mistakes because they attempt nothing. The WINNERS are down in the arena of life, where the action is. A formula I once read for self-renewal stated: "Find something that needs to be done and start doing it." This formula sounds quite simple, but you will find that it will work wonders for you.

After visiting Bombay, India, a past president of Lions International was on a speaking tour in the United States. He related an account of something that members of the Lions Club did for their city of Bombay. One winter night a member awoke chilled from the cold weather. Even though he put more covers on his bed, he could not go back to sleep. Lying there, he thought of the people on the streets who had no home and no cover to help keep them warm. He realized how blessed he was. At 2:00 A.M. he telephoned ten other Lions and told them to bring blankets to those in need. The speaker said in all his life he had never found anything that warmed his heart as the blankets seemed to warm the bodies of those homeless people.

The following affirmations can help us experience more enjoyable and rewarding days.

> Today I am going to take health, happiness, and prosperity to every person I meet.
> Today I will make all my friends feel they are important.
> Today I will look at the sunny side of everything and make my optimism come true.

Today I will think only of the best, work only for the best, and expect only the best.

Today I will forget the mistakes of the past and press on to the greater achievements in the future.

Today I will wear a cheerful countenance at all times and give every living creature I meet a smile.

Today I will give so much time to the improvement of myself that I have no time to criticize others.

Today I will be too large to worry, too noble to be angry, too strong to be afraid, and too happy to permit the presence of trouble.

The next strategy for reaching your potential is to set and achieve goals. I don't know of any corporation, business, or individual who has been successful without having a clear set of goals. WINNERS know where they want to go. And they don't worry about all the methods by which they'll achieve their goals. Many of the methods will develop or unfold as they pursue the goals. I hope you completed the worksheets in chapter 5 concerning your goals.

Goals are not goals until they are written down and have a time frame attached to them. Setting goals has proven to be a powerful motivator for many people. It intensifies the desire to set additional goals and to reach them.

How would you define the word "success"? It has a variety of meanings. Most people define success in terms of money, power, or education. In my judgment, successful people are those who take their abilities and maximize them to achieve their goals and improve the world in which they live. Ask yourself this important question: "Did I get what I wanted in life?" As Plato said, "Take charge of your life. You can do what you will with it."

Booker T. Washington once said, "I have learned that success is to be measured not so much by the position that one has reached, as by the obstacles which have been overcome while trying to succeed."

Who you are is not as important as who you are becoming. Ashley Montague said, "No matter who or what has caused you to become what you are, that does not absolve you from the responsibility of becoming what you ought to be." I like the philosophy of Bobby Knight, the famous basketball coach at Indiana University. He said, "A lot of people have the will to win, but few have the will to prepare."

Prior to his retirement, Charles Kuralt, my favorite television reporter, was interviewing Bonnie Blair at the 1994 Winter Olympics at Lillehammer, Norway after she had won the fifth gold medal in her career. You'll remember that she was the first woman from the United States to win five gold medals. She responded to one of his questions by saying, "All I know is that I love skating." Bonnie had set her goals and strongly committed herself to achieving them. She continued to focus on her goals as she invested the time and energy it required to become a champion . . . a WINNER.

It's important to set goals that matter to us. Like Bonnie Blair, when we love what we're doing, it becomes more enjoyable and rewarding. And we'll probably do a much better job. The time passes faster. We look forward to going to work. We feel better about ourselves as we utilize our talents and time more productively.

The day had started out just like any other working day for flight attendant Barbara Carter. She was thirty, happily married, and had been a flight attendant for nine years. She was scheduled on a morning flight from New York to Las Vegas, with a layover there. That evening after dinner she and a member of the flight crew were returning to the hotel on his motorcycle. A cab came from a side street and hit them broadside. In less than twenty-four hours, her world was turned upside down and her whole future was in doubt. She had never had a broken leg or arm or even stitches in her whole life.

Paramedics arrived on the scene almost immediately, and the injured were rushed to the emergency room of nearby Sunrise Hospital. Dr. Austin Potenza, an orthopedic surgeon, examined Barbara to see what the injuries were. When she regained consciousness, she was told she would lose her right leg. It had been badly mangled in the crash and she was sore all over from the bruises and lacerations that covered her body.

She had hoped the whole experience was just a bad dream and that she would soon wake up. After hearing the alternatives from the doctor, she knew it wasn't. He said she must have the leg amputated or within nine to eleven hours she would die from loss of blood and gangrene. At midnight that same night, Barbara agreed to let Dr. Potenza go ahead with the surgery. Her right leg was amputated just above the knee.

After five days in intensive care, Barbara was moved to a private room. More operations followed. It was a bad time: physical pain, mental anguish, feelings of helplessness and dependence, regret for simple pleasures that would no longer be possible. Worst was her fear of the unknown. She didn't know what to expect from life with only one leg. At times she wondered whether she had made the right decision about allowing the amputation.

At the beginning of her recuperation, she wrote down three goals she wanted to reach: to walk as normally as she could, to play tennis again, and to resume her job as flight attendant. At the time these goals seemed nearly impossible, but she knew she had to strive for them.

With the help of loved ones, Barbara has been able to accomplish all three goals. She came to realize, too, just how short life can be and she tries to do as much as she can every day.

Her experience also changed her life in that she wanted to help others with handicaps like hers. If you look around, there is always someone who is worse off than you.

Being in the Olympics had been a lifelong dream of Becky Clark, an all-county standout in both volleyball and basketball. After high school, she was picked to be the twelfth player on the volleyball squad that would represent the United States in the World Games for the Deaf in Cologne,

Germany. She had no idea she would make the team because she had not played volleyball since high school.

The Deaf Olympics receives no financial backing from the government, AAU, or U.S. Olympics committee. Each athlete must raise his or her own funds to make the trip to Europe. Becky had to raise $4,000. And she did.

Overcoming obstacles was not unusual for this determined twenty-one-year-old. Becky was born with an 18-percent decibel loss but by now she had experienced a 100-percent hearing loss. Her athletic career was filled with challenges. Being deaf was only a part of her many problems. She had suffered from a thyroid condition that required daily medication. A circulation problem forced her to wear medical stockings.

Becky Clark's goal and lifelong dream of being an Olympian is a reality. She doesn't consider herself a handicapped person. She feels that she has the world by the tail. She wants to write a book someday: *The Deaf Athlete.* Another goal is to coach deaf athletes. She feels that she can make a contribution to others because she can relate to some of the problems deaf athletes have.

Winston Churchill's indomitable spirit during the dark days of World War II is reflected in his encouragement to the British people. He said, "Tomorrow will be better. The day will come when we will win. The final victory will be ours." After the war, Churchill was invited to speak to the boys at the school he had attended. The headmaster told the boys to bring notebooks and copy down everything he said because they were to hear the greatest living Englishman. Churchill walked to the platform and looked at their faces. He realized that life would hold many challenges and opportunities for them. His complete speech was, "Never give in, never give in, never, never, never." He then sat down.

What should you do when you reach a "tired spot" in life? Some people rest a while and then get on with the task of living and working. Other people reach a tired spot and quit. They abandon their goals. I like the inspiration in the story of the little girl, Leslie, who was walking home with her father, Chuck Gadd. She became a little tired and asked her dad to carry her the rest of the way home. Chuck was also tired. What should he do? What would you have done? Chuck cut a limb from a tree, handed it to Leslie, and said, "Here's a fine horse for you to ride home." Leslie beat her father home!

That is the way you will find life. Sometimes you are so tired mentally and physically that you will think you can't go on. Then you will find a stick horse—in the form of a friend, a song, a poem, a flower, a baby's smile, or the gentle hand of a spouse—and over the tired spot you will gallop. Look around for your stick horse.

There are often stumbling blocks on the pathway of progress. For generations great leaders, statesmen, astronauts, and inventors have had to overcome obstacles that stood in their way. It has been well said that we stumble over molehills and not mountains. Instead of concentrating on molehills, WINNERS review their goals periodically to keep themselves energized to achieve them.

The poem written by Gail Brook Burkett can help us maintain a proper perspective on the challenges we face.

> I do not ask to walk smooth paths
> Nor bear an easy load,
> I pray for strength and fortitude
> To climb the rock-strewn road.
> Give me such courage that I can scale
> The hardest peaks alone,
> And transform every stumbling block
> Into a stepping-stone.

Now let's turn to the seventh strategy: learning to communicate effectively with yourself and others. Most of all this requires the ability to listen—to ourselves and to others. We are in a continuous dialog with our inner selves. In fact, the most important conversations we have each day are those we have with ourselves. This silent voice is constantly telling us what to do, what not to do, what to say, and what to look for. Our lives are greatly enriched when we feed our inner selves with healthy mental thoughts. You are doing this now as you read this book. You are giving yourself an "inner massage."

Becoming a good listener requires effort. Most of us were born with the ability to hear—we were not born with the ability to listen. Listening is a skill that can be developed. A lot of people have taken courses in public speaking—very few people have taken a course in listening.

Listening is silent flattery. Listening is loving. A research study from Loyola University in Chicago concluded that listening is the single most important characteristic of an effective leader.

Active listening requires that we try to understand through the experiences and values of those to whom we are listening. This is a demanding task. It requires a spirit of objectivity. It is an intense effort to empathize with another, "to walk," as the Indian proverb says, "a mile in his moccasins."

Communicating accurately is a challenging art. It requires the alertness and speed of a swordsman and the sensitivity of an artist. It requires a keen mind, a loving heart, perception, compassion, the ability to paint and praise, as well as the ability to detect and direct.

A woman seeking counsel from Dr. George W. Crane, the psychologist, confided that she hated her husband, and intended to divorce him. "I want to hurt him all I can," she declared firmly. "Well, in that case," said Dr. Crane, "I advise you to start showering him with compliments. When you have become indispensable to him, when he thinks you love him devotedly, then start the divorce action. That is the way to hurt him."

Some months later the wife returned to report that all was going well. She had followed the suggested course. "Good," said Dr. Crane. "Now's the time to file for divorce." "Divorce!" the woman said indignantly. "Never. I love my husband dearly!" When she and her husband began communicating again, love bloomed anew.

You can give more than is expected in your relationship with others by practicing the following "Ten Keys to Happier Human Relations":

1. Speak to people. A cheerful word of greeting will brighten their day.
2. Smile at people. It takes seventy-two muscles to frown—only fourteen to smile. Remember that a smile is a gentle curve that straightens out many things.
3. Call people by name. The sweetest music to anyone's ears is the sound of his or her own name.
4. Be outgoing and helpful. If you want friends, be friendly yourself.
5. Be cordial. Speak and act as if everything you did was a genuine pleasure.
6. Be truly interested in others. You can like nearly everybody if you try.
7. Be generous with praise. Offer specific compliments to others for work well done.
8. Be considerate of the feelings of others. It will be appreciated.
9. Be open to the opinions of others. There are three sides to a controversy—yours, the other person's, and the right one.
10. Be poised to give service. What counts most in life is what we do for others.

If you communicate with others in these compassionate ways, you will be making another great stride towards being a WINNER.

And finally, our last strategy for releasing our

untapped potential is learning to negotiate with the circumstances of living and working. We must develop the flexibility to flow with the tide. We cannot control all things, but we can negotiate most things. And surely we can control our attitudes and reactions to circumstances. It's the person who makes the difference, not the circumstances.

Our society is an information-centered one. Many employees will be retrained during their lifetimes for five or six unrelated jobs. This can cause a lot of trauma for us. And that's why each of us must develop skills and strategies that will help us adapt effectively to appropriate changes.

Some people procrastinate to avoid change. Yet we all know that change is an inevitable part of living. All living things change. We are not the same persons we were last week. And we'll be different next week. A colleague of mine, Dr. Jeff Crabtree, says that the only people who like change are wet babies. I believe that the key to managing change effectively isn't liking it, but understanding it.

Someone said that the three most important rules in life are:

> 1. To go.
> 2. To keep going.
> 3. To help someone else go.

It requires faith to see the undeveloped butterfly in the caterpillar. And it requires faith in ourselves to capture the vision of the people we'd like to be. I hope you will look into the mirror today and see two people . . . the person you are today and the person you intend to become.

In a nursing home in a large northeastern city, two elderly men shared a room. The one in the bed near the window was a heart patient. The other man had a broken hip. Both men were confined to bed. They could not wander around the halls and enjoy the company of some of the other patients living there.

Occasionally, when both of the men were awake, the one located closest to the window would look out and attempt to describe for the other man what was going on in the outside world. Their room was located on the second floor and the man with the broken hip could only see the blue sky.

The dialog would go something like this: "Across the street is a beautiful park. There are lots of people in the park today since the weather is so beautiful. It is a perfect day to be outside." The next day he described the scene in which a lovely nurse, who frequently came to the park about the same time each day, was stopping to talk to many of the people in the park. He said, "You would enjoy watching her as she slowly strolls along the walkway."

As the days went by, the man noticed that a young intern was also coming to the park about the same time as the nurse. He was coming from the opposite direction as they passed each other. It was obvious at first that they did not know one another since they exchanged only a casual glance as they passed. But as the days went on, the man noticed that the two stopped and chatted with one another. Before long this friendship had become more than a casual acquaintance. The couple began to meet regularly about the same time each day for about fifteen minutes, visiting on the park bench.

The man who described the beauty of the fall leaves in the park, the sunsets, the squirrels as they scampered up the trees, the ducks in the pond, and the little children playing, suddenly died of a heart attack. The man who was left in the room asked one of the nurses if he could be moved closer to the window so that he could enjoy the beauty of the park. He missed the daily ritual of being told what was happening there.

That evening toward sunset he lifted himself up in bed so he could view the park and some of the lovely things his friend had described. He was shocked to learn that there was nothing outside that window but a dreary, asphalt-covered parking lot. His friend who had died had taken a joyless situation and turned it into a positive for himself and his roommate.

As you practice the principles of success given in this book, you will display a more positive and radiant attitude and your personality will be so magnetic that more people will want to associate with you. I'd like to close this book by sharing with you an old Irish prayer. It says: "May the road rise up to meet you, may the winds be always at your back, may the sun shine warm upon your face, may the rains fall soft upon your fields, and until we meet again may God hold you in the palm of his hand."

WISDOM FROM WINNERS

WINNERS believe that learning is the one absolutely necessary common denominator of successful people.

WINNERS know that the greatest joys in life come when they are developing their talents and making a positive contribution where they live and work.

WINNERS view pain as inevitable and misery as optional.

WINNERS know that self-pity is the most dangerous emotion and that self-value is the most helpful emotion.

WINNERS know that "the main thing" is to keep the main thing the main thing.

WINNERS believe that success in life is 10 percent of what actually happens to them and 90 percent how they choose to react to it.

WINNERS accept themselves as changing, growing, imperfect human beings.

WINNERS know through their own self-talk that they are either in the construction business or the wrecking business.

ACTION SHEET
"Releasing Your Untapped Potential"

The following paragraph reflects my primary goal in life if I knew that I only had one year to live and that I was guaranteed success in whatever I attempted. Under this paragraph I will draw a picture, design, or symbol that represents my primary purpose in life.

ACTION SHEET
"Releasing Your Untapped Potential"

The following paragraph describes from deep in my heart why I believe I am on this earth. It includes my skills, talents, uniqueness, when I have made a difference, and why I get up in the morning.

ACTION SHEET
"Releasing Your Untapped Potential"

Because the deepest satisfaction comes from making a difference in the lives of others, this week I will develop my "service potential" by practicing "random kindness and senseless acts of beauty" with the following people or situations:

1.

2.

3.

4.

5.

ACTION SHEET
"Releasing Your Untapped Potential"

The following list identifies five positive factors in my life (including people, activities, or anything else) that help to keep me positive, upbeat, and energized. Why?

1.

2.

3.

4.

5.